Charles Woodruff Shields

The Reformer of Geneva

A Historical Drama

Charles Woodruff Shields

The Reformer of Geneva
A Historical Drama

ISBN/EAN: 9783337296445

Printed in Europe, USA, Canada, Australia, Japan

Cover: Foto ©Thomas Meinert / pixelio.de

More available books at **www.hansebooks.com**

The Reformer of Geneva

An Historical Drama

By

Charles Woodruff Shields

Professor in Princeton University

G. P. PUTNAM'S SONS
NEW YORK & LONDON
The Knickerbocker Press
1898

"Post Tenebras Lux."
Motto of Geneva.

The Reformer of Geneva

DRAMATIS PERSONÆ.

AMIED PERRIN. The Captain-General.
PHILIBERT BERTHELIER. A Libertine Courtier.
CLAUDE RIGOT. The Attorney-General.
PIERRE TISSOT. The Lord Lieutenant.
VANDEL. A Senator favoring Perrin.
DU PAN. A Senator favoring Calvin.
D'ARLOD. Lord Syndic and leader of the Majority.
JOHN CALVIN. The Reformer.
NICOLAS DE LA FONTAINE. Secretary to Calvin, and lover of Idelette.
GERMAIN COLLADON. A French Refugee and Lawyer.
FAREL }
POUPIN } Pastors.
BERNARD }
MICHAEL SERVETUS. The Heretic.
WILLIAM GUEROULT. Printer to Servetus.
CLAUDE DE GENÈVE. Jailer and instrument of Perrin.
FRANCESCA. Wife of the Captain-General.
IDELETTE. Their daughter.

The City Herald, the State Secretary, State Messenger, French Papal Envoy, Jailers, Archers, Senators, Citizens, Burghers, Peasants, Artisans, Attendants.

Scene in Geneva. Time, 1553.

ACT I.

THE PLOT OF THE LIBERTINES.

Scene   I.—The Captain-General's Palace.
Scene II.—The Door of the Cathedral.
Scene III.—The Same at Curfew.
Scene IV.—Interior of the Consistory.

ACT I.

SCENE I.

A Room in the Palace of the CAPTAIN-GENERAL. FRANCESCA *and* IDELETTE *are embroidering. The Cathedral bell rings.*

Francesca. Come! there's the bell for vespers, Idelette.
Idelette. No, mother; 't is the evening sermon now.
Francesca. Ah! I forget—No matins and no vespers—
Nothing but sermons, doctrines, all day long.
The very peasants have befogg'd their brains
With wordy talk about the Trinity,
Free-will, Election, what-not—why not leave
Such things to priests?
Idelette. Why not, indeed? And yet
I never liked the filthy priests, nor would
Confess to them.
Francesca. To whom, then, will you go?
Idelette. Alas! to Master Calvin, for some counsel.
Francesca. And little would you get:—a catechism
On the fine points of his divinity;
Some goodish talk about old Jewish saints;
And preachments 'gainst the wickedness of plays,
Cards, dances, and the dire enormity
Of frills and flounces. Child, is thy new gown

The Reformer

Made ready for the fête to-night?
   Idelette.   It seems
I dare not wear it. The Consistory [1]
Has pass'd an edict—
   Francesca.   The Consistory!
Pray, what has the Consistory to do
With thy toilette?
   Idelette. (*Handing a scroll.*) It's in the missive left
By the French gentleman, their Secretary.
   Francesca. What! that young Nicolas de la Fontaine?
How dare he bring to us their pious twaddle!
   Idelette. (*Aside, kissing a letter as she withdraws.*)
Ah! my good mother, something else he brought!
                                   [*Exit* IDELETTE.
[PERRIN *and* BERTHELIER *enter apparently conversing, and
    approach* FRANCESCA *while she peruses the scroll.*
   Francesca. See here, most gallant Berthelier, and you
That are, or seem the Captain-General
Of this proud city and my lord and master,—
What petticoat government we are under!
   [*Reads.*] " It is decreed: No woman in what rank
Or quality soever she may be
Dareth to be so hardy as to make,
Or cause to be made or to wear two flounces
Or more than two, embroider'd, fac'd or lin'd
With silk,—on pain to forfeit sixty sous." [2]
   Berthelier. Ha! ha! our Master Calvin even sets
The fashions for us. Here are other edicts:
   [*Produces a paper and reads.*]
" No man durst wear gay hose or figur'd doublet;
Nor dance with any woman at a fête;
On pain of bread and water for three days."
   Francesca. What a religion! Lent! the whole year
      round.

of Geneva.

Berthelier. (*Reads.*) "Let there be no more games
 —no more stage-plays—
No holidays—sermons on three work-days—
All citizens to be at home for prayers
And lights put out at half-past nine o'clock,
What time the curfew of St. Peter tolls."
 Perrin. Great Cæsar! Who is master in Geneva?
 Berthelier. One of our stately dames has been rebuk'd,
Because her maid had dress'd her coiffure too
Coquettishly for the Consistory.
 Francesca. Ha! ha! Most reverend court of co-
 quetry!
 Berthelier. And a pert, laughing damsel has been
 deem'd
Not good enough to wear a bridal wreath.
 Francesca. "Penthesilea! Queen of Amazons,"[2]
Dares he call me. Oh! would I were a man,
Or might but use the power of you men,
I 'd make this wand'ring preacher stick to his text
And leave us women to our millinery.
 [*Tears the paper to pieces.*]
He calls you "Comic Cæsar."[3]
 Perrin. Comic Cæsar?
By Cæsar! He shall pay dear for that jest.
I yet will play me such a comedy
As he may find a rueful tragedy.
Our friend the noble Berthelier is here
To lay the plot. He comes to talk state matters
With me alone.
 Francesca. (*Withdrawing.*) Choose well your parts,
 my Lords.
 [*Exit* FRANCESCA.
 Perrin. Have we cast off the yoke of dukes and
 bishops

7

The Reformer

But to be rul'd by this evangelist!
    Berthelier.   The dukes, my lord, have had their day,
        because
They colleagued with the bishops: so they fell
Together. Now the burghers lose the game
By calling back this subtle divine from Strasburg
To play the pope among us.
    Perrin.   Not yet: not yet: the noblesse of Geneva
Have not all bowed to the adventurer
From Picardy. 'T is true, we take his creed;—
It's neither French nor Genevese, and suits
The rabble,—But his rule in civic rights
We take not, and will crush his rule in manners.'
    Berthelier.   That's easy said. The banish'd cleric
        comes
With popular gales to waft him back to power.
    Perrin.   But not to grasp quite all the reins of power!
We hold the ancient rights episcopal,
Descended with the ducal to our hands.
    Berthelier.   Perhaps he means to yield the sword of
        State
But keep himself the keys o' the Church : [5]—a game
That he plays well.
    Perrin.   No doubt. But still
We have our curb:—the edict lately pass'd:
No clergy henceforth in the Senate, there
To thwart our counsels and to kill our votes.
    Berthelier.   How stand the new elected senators?
    Perrin.   Most favorably: Vandel, Sept, Defosses,
Des Arts and Favre, men whom we can trust,
Kinsmen or friends of mine, good livers all
And haters of the new ascetic rule.
Our Vandel leads them with his haughty tongue.
    Berthelier.   And how do stand the other senators?

of Geneva.

Perrin. Well,—not so well. Du Pan leads Botellier,
Aubert, Corné, and Lambert; these we know
To be austere and wily puritans.
Fifteen remain to lean to either side.
   Berthelier. Ay, there remain the dangers to the cause.
Our power is based upon the populace,
In both the civic Councils, Great and Small;
And as the city fills with Calvinists,
Exiled from all the provinces of France,
Some day the alien creed may undermine
The whole republic.
   Perrin.   Ah, but you forget,
The Senate has decreed, within the walls,
These dogs of Frenchmen shall not carry arms.[6]
So have we plucked away the serpent fangs
Nurs'd in the gen'rous bosom of the state.
   Berthelier. Most noble lord and Captain-General,
You quite mistake me. These our enemies
Fight not with carnal weapons, as they like
To say,—though well enough they fight with fagots
Among themselves,—their power is in the realm
Of thought and spirit, where no state-craft comes.
Some different doctrine must be sown broadcast.
   Perrin. What! would my lord turn preacher then ?
You speak a riddle.
   Berthelier.   No:—a simple secret;
And a state-secret, if you keep it well.
Know you, there is a preacher come to town,
Not reverend in title, but disguised,
A gallant like ourselves and hidden safe
At the Inn-of-the-Rose, across the Lake,—
One Michael Servetus, the physician,
Known as a sower of great heresies
Through Christendom.[7]

The Reformer

Perrin. Well? more of this state-secret.
Berthelier. He much hath writ against our famed divine,
The printer of his book, William Gueroult,
A sometime banished Libertine, but now
In sheep's clothing, near the sacred pale,
Under the very noses of the pastors spreads
The heresy like murrain through their flocks.
Perrin. But when the shepherds scent the murrain there,
What then?
Berthelier. Why, better, then, for us; and worse
For them—Dissensions in the folds themselves
By two reformers—Power in our hands
To drive one at the other or send both
Of them where they can never plague us more.
Perrin. Bravo! bravo! Not that I care a sou
For either doctrine. Anything to put
This upstart alien down and keep intact
Our civic rights and ancient liberties.
Berthelier. If one must choose, I'd choose the newer doctrine.
Our sham Reformer only half reforms.
His discipline destroys indulgences,
But keeps the old-time penances, and kills
The joy and charm of life while in the bud.
The later gospel of true liberty
Frees both the spirit and the flesh, with all
Their natural and innocent desires;
And so makes full communion of saints
In bodies and in goods as well as souls—
A holy wedlock with a holy kiss.[8]
Perrin. Aha! I see you have the greater stake.
It is a bargain. Philibert Berthelier,

of Geneva.

Son of that sire who freed us from the yoke
Of Savoy, give to me thy hand.
[*They clasp hands.*]   And so
We have the prologue of our "Comic Cæsar."
The play is on. Come, drink success to it.
Long live Geneva!
  Berthelier.   Long live the Libertines!

SCENE II.

Before the ancient Gothic[9] *Doorway of the Cathedral of St. Peter. A Psalm concluding within. Worshippers dispersing. Two Burghers tarry.*

  First Burgher. Well, brother, think you the discourse
    was sound?
  Second Burgher. 'T was meat for men, not milk for
    babes.
  First Burgher.   Too tough
For my digestion, some of it.
  Second Burgher.   By prayer
And meditation only we digest
Sound doctrine.
  First Burgher.   Truly: yet we cannot pray
Against Eternal Will; nor meditate
How Three are One and still One must be Three.
  Second Burgher. And therefore am I for a Trinity.
  First Burgher. And therefore am I for a Unity.
  Second Burgher. Your Unity would be you know not
    what.
  First Burgher. Your Trinity would be a Cerberus.[10]
  Second Burgher. What 's that?

The Reformer

First Burgher. The fabled hell-hound with three heads.
Second Burgher. Flat blasphemy! You ne'er learned
    aught like that
From Master Calvin's sermons or his books.
First Burgher. Oh, there's another doctor now abroad,
Another book beside the *Institutes*.
Second Burgher. What doctor, and what book?
First Burgher.   A doctor learn'd
In new divinity, a second Luther,
Reformer of reformers; and his book,
Sometime to be discreetly shown to you,
Is the quintescence of the faith, distilled
Into a pure " Restored Christianity."
Second Burgher. 'T is heresy! vile heresy! both book
And heretic fit to be burn'd. Look you!
[SERVETUS, *disguised as a Libertine, passes with a gallant
    air.*]
Yon flaunting Libertine!
First Burgher.   A citizen
He seems of gallant mien.
Second Burgher.   Last Sabbath morn,
As Satan came among the sons of God,
Came he into the assembly of the saints,
Affronting them with jewels, gay attire,
And silly foppish airs. Came he to pray,
He must be warned to wear the sober garb
Ordained by the Consistory. Came he
To spy our Canaan out, then as a spy
Shall he be treated. I must hence away
To put the brethren on their guard."   [*Exit.*
First Burgher.   Good soul!
He little deems that flaunting Libertine
The heretic himself, Michael Servetus,
Reformer of this now deform'd Geneva.   [*Exit.*

of Geneva.

SCENE III.

The same transformed by Nightfall. The Curfew tolling. The NIGHT WATCHMAN, *with flambeau, going and returning.*

Night Watch. Past nine o'clock! To prayers! Hie home to prayers!
[*Enter* SERVETUS *and* GUEROULT, *meeting as the Night Watch passes.*
Servetus. (*To* GUEROULT). Off, caitiff, with thy cap, before thy masters.
Gueroult. Our masters force us to be meek and lowly.
Night Watch. The curfew bids you home, good citizens.
Servetus. What if we tarry here?
Night Watch. To prison till
To-morrow morn, and then a reprimand
From the most reverend Consistory.
Gueroult. 'T is better to obey the powers that be.
Night Watch. Past nine o'clock! To prayers! Hie home to prayers! [*Exit.*
Servetus. Is that old prowler out of ear-shot yet?
I sometimes fancy we are dogg'd and watch'd.
Gueroult. He'd never take you for a heretic.
Servetus. He'd never take you for a Libertine.
Gueroult. Now we are safe, unless church walls have ears.
Servetus. How goes the good work on?
Gueroult. Bravely; the book
Is read upon the sly and handed about
And tasted like some titbit.
Servetus. Do the parsons
Suspect it?
Gueroult. Bless you! Pastor Poupin has

The Reformer

A nose for heresy that scented it
As far off as Vienne in Dauphiny,
But does not smell it now under his pulpit.
    Servetus.   And Pastor Bernard?
    Gueroult.   Oh, the more he rails
Against Servetus all the more they read
Servetus.
    Servetus.   And that lying old impostor,
Who answers not my letters?
    Gueroult.   Master Calvin!
Oh, he but writes to princes and grand ladies,
That like to have him for a conscience-keeper.
Why think you we are watch'd?
    Servetus.   The other day
I stroll'd to church—
    Gueroult.   Rash, very rash.
    Servetus.   To hear once more an orthodox discourse.
Methought the brethren look'd askance and eyed
Inquiringly my figured hose and doublet.
    Gueroult.   Did any of them follow you?
    Servetus.   Since then
The landlord of the Inn is very curious.
    Gueroult.   To know you better as a paying guest?
    Servetus.   Oh, no! He slyly asked about my wife.
    Gueroult.   Ha! ha! Your answer?
    Servetus.   That a Libertine
Could take his pleasures as he chose
Without the yoke of marriage.
    Gueroult.   Shrewdly said.
    Servetus.   He also queried of my coming and going.
    Gueroult.   That may have been but mere civility.
    Servetus.   From Spain, I said, to Naples—there to ply
My healing art among the Spanish exiles.
    Gueroult.   Well, that was true enough.

Servetus.   To-morrow I
Shall air my promise, and sail down the lake—[12]
    Gueroult. Returning when the business is more ripe.
    Servetus. Come, come; the moon will soon be up and show
Our faces.
    Gueroult. And our plans, worse than our faces.
                                          [*Exeunt.*

SCENE IV.

The Consistory adjoining the Cathedral. Tomes upon the shelves, the table, and floor. A suspended lamp.
    CALVIN *is dictating to* LA FONTAINE.

    Calvin. How many letters have we, Nicolas?
    La Fontaine. Too many, Sir, to be despatched to-night.[13]
    Calvin. We take the urgent. Name them one by one.
[LA FONTAINE *takes up each letter as he names its purport.*
    La Fontaine. "The Duchess of Ferrara, Italy,"
Sends greetings to her well-remembered friend,
And begs his good advice.
    Calvin.   Ah! brilliant court
Of letters, wit and piety! Brief dream
Of worldly glory not to be! We send
An answer only after thought and prayer
And in most courteous phrase, as shall beseem
This gracious lady.[14] Pass we to the next.
    La Fontaine. "Appeal of Persecuted Protestants
In France." By secret messenger.
    Calvin.   Most urgent.

The Reformer

Our brethren faint and perish. We must write
Before we sleep.
    La Fontaine. "His Grace of Canterbury" bids to
        Lambeth
A Council of Reformed divines, to heal
The broken unity of Christendom.
    Calvin. Mark that "Important, not Immediate."
A noble summons! I would cross ten seas
To answer it. Mayhap, I be not stayed
To heal some deadly breach in our own walls.
    La Fontaine. "Queen Margaret of Navarre" is not
        well pleas'd
To hear that Monsieur Calvin writes a book
Against the sect of Libertines, of whom
She reckons some amongst her chosen friends."[16]
    Calvin. Alas! Madam! though loyal to thy house,
As to all Christian princes, speak I must,
Else I were false to thine own Lord and mine,
Betrayed by those who mask their fleshly sin
In heavenly grace and call that "liberty"
Which is but lust. Even a dog will bark,
Whose master is assail'd.
    La Fontaine.   The next is seal'd
With the great ancient seal of the Republic:
"The noble the Lord Syndics of Geneva
Mandamus to the Reverend Presbytery—"
That certain censur'd Libertines have leave
To take the Holy Supper.
    Calvin. Put that aside for the Consistory.
So falls the first bolt from the low'ring cloud
That gathers over this unhappy Church.
    La Fontaine. "Philip Melancthon, to his Dearest
        Friend
And Brother"—

of Geneva.

Calvin.   That must wait some tranquil hour.
O Philip Melancthon! a hundred times
Upon this bosom hast thou laid thy head,
And pray'd to live and die with me.   Would God
That thou wert near me at this hour!   Afar
Thou watchest now the spiritual combat,
And forward lookest to the Righteous Judge,
Who holds th' unfading wreath for which we strive.[16]
   La Fontaine.   One letter more—a servant maid that craves
A note to Pastor Farel.
   Calvin.   Write at once:
And add a safe-conduct to Neufchâtel.
   La Fontaine.   Another!   An old worn letter, out of date,
Left by an unknown hand, from Michael
Servetus, in Vienne, Province of Lyons:—
Too insolent, I think, for you to read.
   Calvin.   Poor, stiff-necked, crazy heretic!
Throw it unread into the escritoire
With thirty others like it.   [*Loud knocks at the door.*]
                  See who comes.
None but the members of Consistory.
   [*Enter* POUPIN *and* BERNARD, *ushered by* LA FONTAINE.
   La Fontaine.   The reverend pastors Poupin and Bernard.
   Calvin.   Right welcome, brethren.   What good tidings do
Ye bring?
   Poupin.   Most honored master,—only bad:
A wolf is in the fold.
   Bernard.   A pack of wolves!
   Calvin.   Ye speak in proverbs, darkly.

The Reformer

Poupin.   Plainly then:
That compound of all heresy, the Spaniard
Michael Servetus, our worst enemy,
Is in Geneva.
    Bernard.   And the Libertines
Are plotting with him to pull down our Church.
    Calvin.   How came he here?
    Poupin.   Nobody knows. Since he
Escap'd the papal fagots at Vienne,
He has been wandering in Italy
Or France; and now, with that outlaw'd Gueroult,
His secret printer, he has turned up here,
Inside the very portals of the church.
    Calvin.   What fatal madness!
    Poupin.   Madness of long standing.
    Bernard.   The moth into the flame!
    Calvin.   Long since I warn'd him
That if he came he never would depart
Alive." But is there no way out for him?
    Poupin.   None: he leaves none,—he has been sowing tares
Among our wheat for several weeks.
    Bernard.   Is such a murderer of souls to be
Let loose in Christendom?
    Calvin.   Right or wrong,
He must at least be tried. So may we hope
To save him from himself and save the Church.
If he recants, and God shall change his heart,
We cannot but rejoice. If he is punished,
The churches will have rest. If he escapes—
    Bernard.   Can there be any *ifs?*
    Calvin.   The risks are great:—
This Senate lately pack'd with Libertines—
This fickle Council of Two Hundred led

of Geneva.

By crafty Berthelier—this young noblesse
Chafed by our discipline—this furious queen
Penthesilea, with her bacchanals—
This play-house Cæsar, playing government—
And now this crazy heretic come to be
Their tool and leader,—we must look to God,
And set our faces as a flint. Go now;
Keep watch and bring me word of the arrest.
   [*Exeunt the Pastors. Enter* COLLADON *ushered by* LA FONTAINE.
   La Fontaine. Here is our learned Counselor Colladon.
   Calvin. (*Advancing.*) A timely visit in a time of need.
We want the lawyer more than the divine.
   Colladon. Some whisper of this business brings me here.
   Calvin. The case is serious, with but one recourse:—
The law must take in hand the heretic.
   Colladon. You being judge of that—a judgment I
Can but approve—command me, and I serve.
The edicts of the Swiss here govern us;
They have the *Lex talionis*.
   Calvin.   Pray explain.
   Colladon. 'T is written in the Book of Exodus [18]:—
" Thou shalt give eye for eye, and tooth for tooth."
As heresy is spiritual murder, made
In law the highest capital offence,
Th' accuser goes to prison with th' accused,
And puts his life in forfeit, under pain
Of strict retaliation, should he fail
To prove his charge." [18]
   Calvin.   I knew as much. Meanwhile
This pressing work of mine?

The Reformer

Colladon.   As I have said.
The accuser must become a prisoner.
   La Fontaine. (*Starting up.*) Let me be th' accuser
      then. To save
The leader of our Christendom, I go
To prison and to death.
   Calvin.   Brave words, my son.
I knew thee ever quick to sacrifice
Thyself upon the altar of the faith.
   Colladon. The law could not forbid such sacrifice,
Though youth and mercy well might plead against it.
   Calvin. (*Aside to* COLLADON.)
Whoever suffers, he is to be safe.
I see to that.
   Colladon.   Well then; that risk assumed,
Write out the bill of charges in detail
To-night. Inside of four and twenty hours
They must be brought unto the lord lieutenant.
I go at once to get the writ of arrest.   [*Exit.*
   Calvin. Pray, Nicolas, bring to me the books and
      papers
In evidence, as I shall name them; First,
Those ribald letters in the escritoire;
Also, that copy of my *Institutes*,
Soiled with the vomit of his margin notes;
Also the writings of Melancthon, Bucer,
Œcolampadius, Niger, and Capito;
Also, the works of Justin, of Augustine,
And of Tertullian. That is all, Good-night!
Stay: thou hast often noticed the device
Upon my seal."[19]—*A heart held forth as in
The flame of sacrifice:* Remember, since
My first-born went to God, thou art my son.
I pray for thee to-night even in my dreams.

of Geneva.

[*Exit* La Fontaine

[*He goes to the table and writes.*]
  "These are the accusations to be brought
Against the Spaniard, Michael Servetus,
Guilty of heresy, of blasphemy,
And of disturbing Christendom."
  [*After a pause.*]   O God!
What tragedies may not this conflict breed
To our posterity in after-times!" [20]

ACT II.

THE COUNTERPLOT OF THE REFORMERS.

    Scene   I.—The Garden near the Palace.
    Scene II.—The Same by Moonlight.
    Scene III.—Anteroom in the Palace.
    Scene IV.—Interior of the Consistory.

ACT II.

SCENE I.

The Garden of the Palace. Night. Torch bearers, Masquers, with PERRIN, FRANCESCA, BERTHELIER, VANDEL, *and Revellers, opening the Fête.*[1]

Francesca. Ha! ha! no woman dares to wear two flounces!
Vandel. Nor any man gay hose or figured doublet!
Perrin. (*Mimicking* CALVIN.)[2] "Let there be no more plays."
Francesca.   Except the play
Of Cæsar Comicus.
Perrin. (*Mimicking* CALVIN.) "And no more dances."
Francesca. Except the dance Penthesilea leads
Her crew of bacchanals.
Perrin. (*Mimicking* CALVIN.) "And no more games."
Berthelier. Except the game which Master Calvin tries
Betwixt the Huguenots and Libertines.
No dances, games, and plays? Aha! We shall see.
[*Sings, all joining in the chorus.*]

    Life is but a Dance
    Through the whirling hours

The Reformer

Ending in a trance
  Of its jaded powers.
    Trip it lightsomely,
    Hail! true Liberty.

Life is but a Game,
  And the stake is high.
'T is a fickle dame
  Holds the fateful die.
    Toss it recklessly,
    Hail! true Liberty!

Life is but a Play;
  Each must act his part:
Sporting life away
  Is its highest art.
    Play it merrily,
    Hail! true Liberty!

Dances, games and plays;
  Love and wine and song—
These shall fill our days,
  Thro' our whole life long.
    Bid all scruples flee!
    Hail! true Liberty!   [*Exeunt.*

SCENE II.

The same. Moonrise, revealing Lake Leman and the distant Alps. Muffled music of the fête near by. LA FONTAINE *and* IDELETTE *meeting.*

La Fontaine. My Idelette!
Idelette.   I have been waiting long.

of Geneva.

La Fontaine.   Our grave Consistory was late to-night.
Idelette.   Not later than these wanton revellers.
La Fontaine.   From such extremes of grave and gay
    we come
Into this heaven of love, where vows are chaste
As the Alpine moon and hearts transparent
As this dreaming lake.
Idelette.   (*Brief twilight.*)   But look! there is a cloud
Upon the moon, a shadow in the lake.
La Fontaine.   And now the cloud has passed, the
    shadow gone.
The earth and sky are bright again.
Idelette.   Sometimes
The future of our love, so pure and sweet,
Seems to me all too dreamy for this world.
La Fontaine.   That was the shadow of the passing
    cloud.
Still let us keep the faith of happy lovers,
Until we come into the light again.
Idelette.   I dread my father's frown, my mother's rage.
He hates the Frenchman; she, the Huguenot.
He says this Calvin is the French Reynard,
Who came to steal away our liberties,
And mimics his long face and solemn drawl
Until the table roars.[2]   She calls him " Cain "
For Calvin; bids street urchins set their curs
Upon him; mingle cat-cries with his curfew,
And fire off blunderbusses at his door.
She says our roist'ring, pleasure-loving Swiss
Disturb his nerves with so much revelry.
At church she lolls and yawns and rolls her eyes.
She had a placard fastened to his pulpit
In sermon time, which cost a gallant's head.[3]
To hate him is a part of her religion.

The Reformer

    La Fontaine. And what is thy religion, Idelette?
    Idelette. Ah! It's a simple thing of trust and hope.
With neither priest nor preacher moulding it,
I could not choose but make thee my confessor,
And take my sermons only from thy lips.
Easy it was to share thy faith and love,
And sweet it is to mingle prayers and vows.
    La Fontaine. Idelette, I must tell thee something now,
Thou mayst not fully understand as yet.
We soon shall go into the passing cloud
And seem to lose each other for a while.
    Idelette. What! wilt thou leave Geneva?
    La Fontaine.   No; not that.
An evil man with evil words has crept
Among the brethren; and my loving master
Has work for me to do, which will be long,
And may be perilous.
    Idelette.   Oh! I like not much
Your Calvin, with his harsh and bitter tongue
Against the heretics, and sermons cold
And lofty as those peaks of snow, that seem
So far off from our lowly lives; albeit
Sometimes a sad, sweet smile lights up his face,
As if caught from that other world of his,
When at the font he takes the little children
And blesses them.
    La Fontaine.   At such times have you seen
What is but seldom shown, his inner self,
Masked in the courtly scholar and divine
And gentle as a woman or a child.
As most men see him, he is mailed and nerved
To fight the battles of the Lord in times
Of evil strife. His keen retorts are like

A fencer's thrusts at error; and he writes
His creed, as with a pen of flame, upon
The hearts of princes. Some day he will save
Geneva; and Geneva save the Church,
Thence to give truth and freedom to the world.
   Idelette. Well, whoso loves Geneva, him I'll like.
   La Fontaine. And I will love Geneva's fairest flower,
My Alpine rose! my own sweet Idelette!
   [*Enter* PERRIN *and* BERTHELIER, *with some Revellers.*
      IDELETTE *quickly veils herself.*
   Perrin. Ho! ho! What lovemaking have we here?
   Berthelier. Aha! 'T is Nicolas de la Fontaine!
So Master Calvin trains his saintly pupils.
What pretty jade is this? [*Tries to draw her veil.* LA
    FONTAINE *springs toward him and they draw
    swords.*
   Perrin. Peace! Stop these brawlers.
   [*They are separated.*]
Boy, boy, put back thy sword, or give it me.
Didst thou forget: no Frenchman draws his sword
Within Geneva save to perish by it?
   La Fontaine. I do remember, and to thee alone
I yield it; but to any other, never!
                   [*Turns on his heel and goes.*
   Berthelier. As hot in temper as in love. It were
A pity to have spilt such rash young blood.
   Perrin. More pity it's in such a race and creed.
For this bold trespass the philandering saint,
Like any common sinner, must account.
   Berthelier. There is some mystery here to be unveiled.
                 [*Looking toward* IDELETTE.
   Perrin. And now, my pretty one, we take thee back
Into the dance, near to thine elders, where
Thou shalt be safer than with this young stranger.

[IDELETTE *unveils to her father.*
Perrin. My daughter! Idelette! Idelette!
[PERRIN *leads her away, the others rushing out after* LA
    FONTAINE, *with outcries :*
Dog! Frenchman! Calvinist! Kill him!

SCENE III.

*Anteroom in the Palace. Morning. Perrin enters
excitedly, throwing down* LA FONTAINE'S *sword.*

Perrin. " The Play-house Cæsar! " Ay, a farce indeed;
A tragic farce and comic tragedy !
[*Enter two of the Revellers.*]
What! Did ye not take him ?
First Rev.   He was too fleet
For us.
Second Rev. Cur that he is, he slunk away
Into the darkness.
First Rev.   With his tail between
His legs.
Second Rev. Well, we did not see his legs.
French legs, when young, are swift and nimble.
 First Rev. And Genevese legs, when drunken, are
  unsteady.
 Perrin. Have done with all this fooling. Where is
  he ?
 Second Rev. That is a secret which the night has
  hidden.
 Perrin. Zounds! How ye waste the time with words!
  Go straight
Unto the lord lieutenant; bear from me

of Geneva.

As the chief Syndic, orders to search out
And seize one Nicolas de la Fontaine,
Alive or dead; and if alive, have him
Forthwith confined and bound on mortal charge,—
An alien bearing arms within the city walls;
And keep this captur'd sword as evidence [*handing him the sword*].
We soon shall see if there is power enough
In our high office to bring forth this stripling.
 [*Enter* FRANCESCA.   [*Exeunt the Revellers.*
 Perrin. Madame, where now is Idelette?
 Francesca.   Where else
But in her chamber could she be, my lord?
 Perrin. Where else? Last night she could be somewhere else.
To-day—the devil only knows where else!
 Francesca. My lord, you do yourself and me no honor
By such sallies.
 Perrin.   No honor will be left
To us, unless we part these puling fools.
I little dream'd a daughter of this house
Could e'er go moonstruck with a Frenchman.
 Francesca. I little dreamed a daughter of this house
Could e'er go moonstruck with a Calvinist.
She gets it not from me; nor from the Favres,
Who hate the alien creed more than the Perrins
Can hate the alien race. Hast thou forgot
The day my valiant Sire defied the rule
Of this proud preacher, and with cries of " Freedom!"
Was borne to prison, while his son-in-law,
Clad in his shirt, with candle in his hand,
Followed the meek-eyed parsons through the streets '—
Fit prelude to his now eloping daughter?

The Reformer

Perrin.   Well, well; enough of this. How did she take
Your chiding?
   Francesca.   Like a Perrin, for a while.
Until my storm of words was spent, she wept
And sobbed; then wept again; and then
Grew hard and silent as a stone. And now,
I think, her pretty demure face but hides
Some flinty purpose.
   Perrin.   Then she must be warned.
Go bring her hither that she may confront
The other culprit.   [*Exit* FRANCESCA.
   [*Enter* BERTHELIER.
   Perrin.   The ever welcome Berthelier!
How goes our little play?
   Berthelier.   As good as a play,
The plot thickens.
   Perrin.   Is it comic or tragic?
   Berthelier.   Neither; yet both. As you foresaw, these dogs
Of Frenchmen have smelt out the heretic,
And in full cry are on the heresy hunt.
   Perrin.   On the right track?
   Berthelier.   They have their game in bounds.
Servetus, by some freak of folly, went
To church; his gay disguise but marked him out;
The brethren watch'd and track'd him to the Inn,
Where he was straightway seized on capital charge
Of heresy.
   Perrin.   And the accuser who?
   Berthelier.   In fact, our Master Calvin; but in law,
His pupil, De la Fontaine, as a scape-goat
Magnanimously put forth in his stead,
And safely jailed on forfeit of his life.

Perrin.   Hero of last night's escapade?
Berthelier.   The same.
Perrin.   Ha! Now we have both of them where we
   want them.
The Spaniard is our club to beat the Frenchman;
And the same double blow which frees the State
Shall free my house from intermeddlers—
We must away at once to push this business.
   [*Enter* FRANCESCA *with* IDELETTE.]
Madame, the cause of your coming is met
By our going.   State-secrets call me hence,
The which disclos'd shall bring to a safe end
This trouble of our house.   Enough to say,
That smart young Frenchman is in prison now
On forfeit of his life.
                  [*Exeunt* PERRIN *and* BERTHELIER.
   Francesca.   The Blessed Virgin
Be ever praised!   And all the saints, that pluck
Us from the gulf which yawned to swallow up
Our honor.   Go, false daughter of Geneva!
Weep, if thou wilt, thy folly and its fall:
Thou canst not weep a fallen, ruin'd house.
                           [*Exit* FRANCESCA.
   Idelette.   Now have we gone into the passing cloud,
And lose each other in its thickest gloom.
But I will force a way into the light.
Somehow my Nicolas shall yet be free!   [*Exit.*

SCENE IV.

The Consistory. Morning. CALVIN *Studying. Enter* FAREL

   Calvin.   Ah! brother Farel! all goes well, I trust,
At Neufchâtel.

The Reformer

Farel. Ay, well enough. What news
Here in Geneva?
　Calvin. A delicious bit
I heard last night, at billiards with the seigneurs.
Our Bonnivard has taken his fourth wife.
The town is laughing at the dear old priest.
But we forgive the prisoner of Chillon [*]
As many wives as he had years of durance.
Ha! ha! he uses his full liberty.
　Farel. Why not? Old men, who once were priests, have earn'd
Home life and joy as part of our Reform.
　Calvin. Take care, good brother, our Reform end not
Too often in these marriage comedies.
　Farel. Some other news more serious I hear—
Our enemy Servetus in our hands.
　Calvin. Say, rather, in the hands of law and justice.
　Farel. 'T is a most admirable Providence.
Will he repent? that were too much to hope.
Hostile to Christ and cruel to His Church
Will be the judges, if they stay their hands.
Shall petty altar-thieves be put to death,
And murderers that kill men's souls go free?
　Calvin. I hope the sentence may be capital:
Th' atrocious penalty I would remit.[*]
　Farel. What! treat your worst enemy as your friend?
　Calvin. I have no private grudge—and never had—
Yet shrink not from the Master's public call:—
That call which brought me here, as by a hand
Reach'd down from heaven, with your prophetic curse
Upon my love of studious repose:—
That call which held me here among the foes
Of virtue, even while their swords were flashing
Around our pulpits, till a hooting mob

Escorted us beyond the city gates:—
That call which forced me back from happy exile,
From learning, friendship, ease, and growing fame,
A second Jonah to this Nineveh.
Here have I come as to a bleeding cross;
Here have I offered up my heart to God;
Here will I stay and face a hundred deaths,
Rather than yield my flock to ravening wolves.
Whate'er befalls this troubler of our peace,
The Church at any hazard must be saved.

    Farel. But not by weak and foolish clemency.
Look at that insolent heretic Bolsec!
Banished, he only used his liberty
To spoil the Church and ruin helpless souls.
How often have I said no death would be
Too frightful for me, if I taught false doctrine.
I cannot judge Servetus otherwise.   [*Exit* FAREL.

    Calvin. (*Alone.*) Farel, thou judgest with impetuous mind,
Which later thought will temper to more kindness.
God knows I never hated, scarce despised
This rash, hot-headed Spaniard, who so long
Hath striven to mix me up with his wild dreams.
Yet were I made of iron not to feel
His railings at all saving truth and grace,
And blind with folly not to see the ruin
He would pull down both on himself and us,
With myriads of other helpless souls.
'T is Mercy's self that cries aloud to Justice,
As voic'd by prophet and evangelist,
Against a foe of God no less than man.
O why has He who made us to be like
Himself, exacted such severity,
But that His glory may shine forth in us,

The Reformer

T' eclipse our native weakness and blot out
The merely human from our memories!—
Pride—Passion—Pity; kneel ye all to Him,
Sole absolute Right! pure Reason Infinite!
Eternal Will! that rules all other wills
And moulds and nerves them to its high decrees.'
   [*Returns to his Studies.*]
So do perplexities thicken with our cares.
Books, sermons, lectures, letters all confused.
How I miss Nicolas!—[*A knock is heard.*] A gentle knock
As if it were some gentle visitor.
   [*Goes to the door and admits* IDELETTE.]
   Idelette.   Father, I only come as to the priest.
   Calvin.   Daughter, confess to God, and not to man.
Freely thou hast my counsel with my prayer.
   Idelette.   Such help I crave and other help may give
To thee, and to this young French gentleman—[*hesitating*
   Calvin.   Nicolas de la Fontaine, whom I call
My son?
   Idelette.   —Pursued by revellers last night—
   Calvin.   Pardon; mayhap thou speakest of some friend
Not known to me; if of my son, he now
Is safe from such pursuers.
   Idelette.   Not in prison?
   Calvin.   In prison; but by his own act, as soon
The city shall be told, to do a work
Of justice for the Church, most generous,
Not perilous.
   Idelette.   They said his life was forfeit!
   Calvin.   In their eyes forfeit: not in mine. His life
Is safe as thine, and safer far than mine.
Whoever is in peril, he is safe.

of Geneva.

If thou dost think of such a prisoner,
Fear not for him; fear only for the Church,
The exiled Church that he and I would save.
   Idelette. Father, I am a daughter of Geneva:
Henceforth this exiled Church shall be my mother;
Her people be my people; and her God,
My God.
   Calvin. Doubt not, my daughter, that her God
Shall bless thee, and her people cherish thee.
Nor fear aught strange or alien in her welcome.
Since hapless France has spurned her truest sons
And left them only citizens of Heaven,
Geneva is the city of my heart,
That is to be the city of our God
And capital of a new Christendom.⁸
   Idelette. Somewhat of these high things I understand,
And more may learn hereafter.
   Calvin.   Easily
May they be learn'd by simple, trusting souls.
God hath not chosen the mighty and the wise
To be His children, but the childlike, pure
In heart, and ever open to His truth.
Of such is heaven itself; and their good angels
Do always guide them.—Go not out that door.
   [*Opens another door communicating with the Cathedral.*]
Come through the church; and when thou passest where
The ancient altar stood, kneel there and pray
For thy Geneva.
   Idelette.   And for the exiled Church!
   [*Through the open door, she is seen kneeling in the distant
     window light.*
   Calvin. A daughter of Geneva! Something in
Her face I saw, above our maidens,—yet
Like them. And does she know my Nicolas?

ACT III.

THE TRIAL OF SERVETUS.

SCENE I.—A DUNGEON IN THE OLD BISHOP'S PALACE.
SCENE II.—A HALL OF JUSTICE IN THE SAME.

ACT III.

SCENE I.

A Dungeon in the old Bishop's Palace. A window with shelf in view. Enter the Jailer, CLAUDE DE GENÈVE, *with* SERVETUS.

Claude. Thou lookest the most gallant prisoner
That ever came to pine within these walls.
   Servetus. I look not all I may be. [*Handing his sword.*
   Claude. Art thou not
A soldier?
Servetus. Keep these trinkets and this gold
Safely, as listed by your lord lieutenant:—
One hundred crowns; a chain worth twenty more;
Six jeweled rings, one large turquoise, a ruby,
A sapphire, diamond, emerald of Peru:—
Beside this signet ring of coraline.'
   Claude. Ah! thou 'rt a courtier?
   Servetus. Only a physician,
A scholar, and somewhat of a divine.
   Claude. They call'd thee "heretic," "blasphemer," "dog."
   Servetus. I'll call them worse names when we fight with words.
   Claude. And this young Frenchman here in the next cell
Accuses thee?

The Reformer

  Servetus.   Not he: a catspaw he
Of that old lying tyrant, Master Calvin.
  Claude. Gramercy! how these brethren love one
    another!
  Servetus. Pray, leave me. I would be alone.
  Claude. (*Bowing low.*)   I have
My orders from the Captain-General
To humor thee with certain privileges,
That may befit so learn'd a prisoner. [*Exit* CLAUDE.
  Servetus. What privileges in this hateful place?
So ends my vision of a new reform!
Almost within my reach it vanishes.
An outlaw hunted throughout Christendom,
Escaping from the dungeon, rack, and flame,
Have I at last been driven like a rat
Into this hole, here but to rot and die?
May God confound these tyrants of the Church!'
  [*Raps are heard on the window bars.*]
What's that? Who's there?
  Gueroult. (*Appearing at the window.*) Your caitiff
    Libertine!
  Servetus. Halloa! William Gueroult. What brings
    you here?
  Gueroult. The grace of Madame Perrin, and therewith
Some prison fare,—[*Hands in fruit and wine.*
  Servetus.   For which I thank her grace.
  Claude. And likewise good cheer from her doughty
    lord,
Our trusty Captain-General, who thinks
A Spaniel good enough to chase away
The "French Reynard."
  Servetus.   What if Reynard should turn
And rend the Spaniel? It's a dang'rous game.
  Gueroult. Ay, and the danger thickens with the plot.

of Geneva.

Orders have come to have the men enrolled
In fifties, sworn and arm'd with hidden daggers;
Each wearing on his cuirass a white cross,³
To be the sign of his most Christian mission.
   Servetus. What mission? When?
   Gueroult.   Perchance, some Sunday morn,
When the Great Bell from out St. Peter's tower
With solemn peal that is to be their knell,
Is calling forth the alien hordes to church,—
Our wolves, disguised, shall enter with the sheep,
And while the silly flocks are in the heaven
They dream of, shall their dismal psalms be turned
To shrieks, and everywhere the white cross gleam
Above their puddled blood,—old men and youths
And babes and maidens, the whole vermin breed
Must be stamped out and utterly extinct,
Ere this infested city can be free.⁴
   Servetus. The end seems good; the means more
      questionable.
   Gueroult. Your meek divines may settle that. I am
A printer, not a theologian.
But yonder comes our noble Berthelier
To tell you more of this inside. Adieu;
Until we meet outside with freer tongues.
                                    [*Exit* GUEROULT.
   Servetus. So at the darkest comes a gleam of dawn.
Would I were what this jailer took me for,
The soldier more than the philosopher!
   [*Re-enter* CLAUDE, *ushering* BERTHELIER.
   Claude. My orders were to grant some privileges:—
Here is a most distinguished visitor.   [*Exit* CLAUDE.
   Berthelier. Well, Doctor, not so pleasant as the Inn—
But martyrs have had worse accommodation,
                                      [*looking around*]

The Reformer

And from this worse we may proceed to better.
    Servetus. But why this worse? Why tear me from
        my plans
Ere they were ripe?
    Berthelier.   Upon that text I come
To preach to you. Take wisely the wise counsel
Of friends in power, who only wish you well.
    Servetus. I can but be their willing instrument.
    Berthelier. This portrait first behold, as in a glass:—
A stranger knowing little of Geneva,
A scholar knowing less of men than books,
And a reformer with more zeal than knowledge,
Such as this stranger and this scholar lacks.
Add now a nature quick, impetuous, proud;
Chaf'd by a long defeat and desperate,
Yet simple and unguarded as a dupe,
And with one domineering aim possessed
As with a devil;—there you have the portrait.
    Servetus. It's somewhat rudely drawn, but like
        enough.
Now for the sermon.
    Berthelier.   'T will be brief and plain.
Patrons you have among the senators,
And in the city secret followers.
As knowing this, be cool and self-contained:—
The storm will be the fiercer when it bursts.
The judges hear you have been turbulent:—
Hide your proud aims in meek simplicity.
Deny each charge presented without proof:—
Who of us has a right to the whole truth!
I will be at your elbow, as a friend,
To speak for you, should any need arise.
Meanwhile, the hidden leaven of your book
Is working with a yeast of revolution.

of Geneva.

The Council of Two Hundred in a ferment
Will rally at my call with our brave Captain,
Around the martyr-hero of the hour,
And in the whirlwind of o'erturned affairs,
Even as a leaf is caught up in the storm,
You shall be carried to high place and fame.
As soon as Gueroult musters forth his bands,
Our Claude shall bring you word [5]—And so farewell.
                              [*Exit* BERTHELIER.
  Servetus. Good counsel which I take in my own sense.
These noble friends have aims; and I have aims;
And all of us aim at one common foe,
The tyrant ruler of both Church and State.
My secret prayers and lifelong vows, it seems,
Express to them more diabolic zeal.
Well, there are devils on the other side;
And ev'n as Michael fought in heaven, will I,
A Michael, fight this dragon in the Church.[6]

SCENE II.

A Hall of Justice in the old Bishop's Palace. Enter the City Herald, the Lord Syndic D'ARLOD, *Eight* SENATORS *as Assessory Judges, including* DU PAN, VANDEL, BERTHELIER; *the Attorney-General* RIGOT, *the Secretary of Justice. All taking their places as in a Tribunal.* COLLADON *with* LA FONTAINE *and his Jailer; and* TISSOT *in waiting with* SERVETUS *and his Jailer and Guards.*

  Herald. The High Court of Geneva sits in judgment.
  D'Arlod. Call the accuser and the prisoner.

The Reformer

Herald.   The accuser, Nicolas de la Fontaine!
Colladon.   (*Coming forward with* LA FONTAINE *and his Jailer.*)
So please your worships, he is here and ready.
Herald.   The prisoner accused, Michael Servetus!
Berthelier.   The Lord Lieutenant comes with him.
D'Arlod.   Make way!
Tissot. (*Entering with* SERVETUS, *Jailer, and Guards.*)
I have examined well this prisoner,
And find the charges due in law and fact.
D'Arlod.   Then we will hear the deed of accusation.
The Secretary.   (*Reads.*)   " Here in your presence,
   most redoubtable lords,
" Comes Nicolas de la Fontaine, of St. Gervaix
" Au Vixen, France, on forfeit of his life,
" To be accuser of this prisoner,
" Michael Servetus, of Arragon in Spain,
" For deadly heresies which he hath sown
" Through Christendom these more than twenty years,
" In cruel murder of unhappy souls:—
" For blasphemies which he hath writ 'gainst God,
" More horrible than any crimes 'gainst man;—
" And for sedition secretly infused
" Within this church and city of Geneva,
" To whelm the State in bloody anarchy.
" And if these charges be found good and true,
" And you do judge the said Servetus guilty:
" Then the accuser humbly prays he may
" Be spared all further injury and risk
" Of life, and your Attorney-General
" Take up the 'plaint and further prosecute it.
" Not that he shuns a cause all Christians should
" Maintain ev'n unto death, but he hath learn'd
" Such is the ancient custom of your city,

of Geneva.

"And it belongs not unto him to take
"The Office and the duty of another."

Colladon.   Here are the Queries.
[*Hands a roll to* TISSOT.]
                              Let him not mock God
And your Lordships with vague and false replies.

D'Arlod.   Servetus, on your oath to God and man,
True answers make before this righteous court.
We hear you have been turbulent.   You come
As but an old offender heralded.
Ill rumor should be killed outright with truth,
As kings kill graceless messengers of evil.

Tissot.   (*Reads.*)   "Some years ago in Germany there
       was
A book of dreadful blasphemies condemn'd."

Servetus.   'T is true that I did print a little book,
Not blasphemous, and not condemn'd in court.

Colladon.   Only because 't was never brought in court.

Du Pan.   Say you the book contained no blasphemies?

Servetus.   If any can be found, I will correct them.

Tissot.   (*Reads.*)   "Again in Strasburg and in Italy
There was another execrable book,
Which caused no end of trouble."

Servetus.   I did print
Another little book, but never heard
That it caused trouble.

Du Pan.   But why another?
The Doctors had reproved you for the first,
Œcolampadius, Niger, Bucer, Capito?

Servetus.   Most noble lord, by long and deep re-
       search
Into the Holy Scriptures and Church Fathers
I gained new light, not to be hid, we're told,
Under a bushel: and I meant no harm,

The Reformer

Nor have I anywhere been turbulent.
   Du Pan.   Oh, you knew well enough all Christendom
Would be disturbed!
   Servetus.   With but a few divines
In Germany I have discuss'd these matters:
In France, for years, I spoke not to a soul.
   Du Pan.   Ah! there you hid your light under a
      bushel!
   Colladon.   You see with what repute he comes to us.
But there are other charges nearer home.
   Tissot.   (*Reads.*)   "Through many years he hath
      assail'd the Church
And Pastors of Geneva."
   Colladon.   Here are letters
To Pastor Poupin full of vile abuse:
He says our Church is going to the devil!
   Servetus.   I only used the strong polemic terms
Scholastic doctors use.   The same they us'd
Against me, both in Latin and in French.
   Colladon.   Here is our honour'd Calvin's work, be-
      smear'd
With notes too filthy to be read aloud.
   Servetus.   Your Calvin injur'd me in printed books.
My written notes but show where he has err'd.
   Colladon.   Here is his own most revolutionary book,
His so-call'd "New Restored Christianity."
   Servetus.   'T is so called, not because there were no
      truths
But many errors since the time of Nice.
   Tissot.   (*Reads.*)   "The Papal Court of Vienne hath
      adjudg'd
His book destructive of the common faith."
   Servetus.   That charge came from your Calvin, through
      De Trie.

No thanks to him I was not burn'd alive.⁹
The priests let me escape.
   Colladon.   Why came he hither ?
   Tissot. (*Reads.*)   "He hath been leagu'd with other heretics,
In Frankfort, Venice, and in Genoa,
And hither comes to sow his heresies."
   Servetus.   A trav'ler I was passing through your city,
And meant next day to sail across the Lake.
   Du Pan.   Ha! ha! You spent a month in passing through!
   Colladon.   What was he doing at the Inn-of-the-Rose ?
   Tissot. (*Reads.*)   "While at the Inn he air'd some vile amours,
Which are the natural fruit of heresy."
   Servetus.   Oh, that was all the merest pleasantry.
I could not be a libertine if I would,¹⁰
And have liv'd purely as a Christian should.
   Tissot. (*Reads.*)   "With certain traitors here he hath conspir'd;
Chiefly that outlaw'd fornicator, Gueroult,
The printer of his book."
   Servetus.   Oh—ay—no—he
Did understand not that which he had printed.
Nobody do I know in all your city.¹¹
   Colladon.   Enough! enough on that point! Come we now
Unto the kernel charge of heresy.
Wind not around it with mere sinuous words,
But let us have straight answers, Yes or No.
   [CALVIN *appears with the* PASTORS, *behind* COLLADON.
   Tissot. (*Reads.*)   "He calls the Trinity a Cerberus;
Makes ev'n the devil part of Deity;
Says there could be no more of incarnation

The Reformer

In men than asses, and——"
    Berthelier. (*Interrupting.*) Good my Lord Lieutenant,
Pray do be simply just and read no more.
These tropes and figures of polemic wit,
Stript of their prickly husk of verbiage,
Will yield the fruit of truth which I maintain;
And so befriend this friendless prisoner."
    Calvin. (*Advancing beside* La Fontaine.)"
Most honored lords, I crave your pardon, while
I claim my right to be th' accuser here.
Not on this noble youth, but on my head
Be all the peril as I now confront
Not merely this new heresy in the Church,
But come to charge thee, Philibert Berthelier,
With treason to the State!
    Berthelier.   And I hurl back
The charge as a spent javelin to smite
Its owner.
    Vandel. It 's false!
    Du Pan.   It 's true!
[*Cries of* "True!" *and* "False!"
    D'Arlod. (*To the* Herald.) Bid silence.
    Herald.   Silence! Silence!
    D'Arlod. Or true or false, it is beside the point.
Let the attorney speak, as to this prisoner.
    Rigot. What need of words? He hath condemn'd
        himself
In open court, and to his other crimes,
Sedition, blasphemy, conspiracy,
Now addeth perjury to cap his guilt.
A troubler throughout Christendom; long
A secret foe of our republic; here
He hides, a lurking spider, with his web
Of heresy through Italy and France.

of Geneva.

Let web and spider both be swept away,
As with the avenging besom of the Law.
  Du Pan. Away with him!
  Senators.   Ay! Ay!
  D'Arlod.   The Senate wills it,
Most learned Rigot; and through you its mouth
The city now becomes the prosecutor
For its own welfare, peace, and dignity."
  Colladon. And what of him who for the city's life
Hath risk'd his own ? Set forth the law, I pray you,
As to th' accuser.
  Rigot.   He is more than free.
The freedom of the city he hath sav'd
From peril he may claim his own by right,
And share the civic honor he hath won.
  D'Arlod. 'T is so decreed. Give him his sword again,
A trophy twice his own. Enroll his name,
Defender of the city. Go; brave youth,
Begirt with all the power of Geneva,
As free as any of her free-born sons,
And radiant with honor.   [*Handing the sword.*
  Senators.   Vive La Fontaine!
  [*Exit* LA FONTAINE, *with* COLLADON].
Let Master Calvin wait our summons here,
With these expert divines, to probe and cut
The cancer of this fest'ring heresy."
  [CALVIN *and the* PASTORS *withdraw.*]
Look to your prisoner, Lord Lieutenant. Take
Him hence and keep him close with sentries,
And windows barr'd against his plotting allies.
  [BERTHELIER *whispers to* SERVETUS, *as he is about to withdraw with* TISSOT.
  Berthelier. First let us hear what he will say to us.

The Reformer

Servetus.   Most wise, most mighty, most illustrious
　　　lords,
I seek but justice through your clemency;—
That justice of the holy fathers, who
Deem'd heresy a sin 'gainst God and not
A crime 'gainst man, with bloody penalties.
Should so divine a thing as Christian truth
Be dragged into a prison and a court?
If I am wrong, ye need but prove me so
By force of reason and by Holy Writ.[16]
Let not this fierce pursuer seek to write
His tenets in my blood, but bid him come
Before a full assembly of the Church
With weapons spiritual, with texts and proofs:
There let us have our wordy battle out
And by the issue will I stand or fall.[17]
　Calvin. (*Returning.*) No higher honor could this
　　　court confer
Than bid me so defend my Master's cause,
With all the people witnesses and judges.
　　　　　　　[*Exeunt* CALVIN *and* PASTORS.
　Vandel.   He were ill-match'd against this sharp
　　　polemic.
　Du Pan.   It might be well to have his errors shown
In fair debate upon the public stage.
　D'Arlod.   No; no: this trial is no mere debate:
We must not make a show of law and justice
Before a gaping crowd.
　Rigot.　　　　　Nor dare we yield
To this adventurer, who would seduce
And stir the people up to mutiny.
He plead for canon law and precedent
Who as a schoolboy read Justinian
Denouncing death to all such heretics?

of Geneva.

He prate of his offence as spiritual?
And cite us to a wordy tournament
As though we were a synod of divines?
We charge him with a crime as well as sin:
No subtle heresy of thought alone,
To rend the minds of men apart; nor yet
Mere blasphemy to shock the highest Heaven
And jar the base of order here on earth,
But that dire scourge alike of Church and State,—
Sedition, with wild eyes and flaming torch,
And riot, rapine, ruin in its train.
  [*Pointing towards* BERTHELIER *and* SERVETUS *who are
    seen whispering together.*]
And must we add?—some whisper'd treason there!
  Servetus. My lords, I am a poor, lone stranger here,
Unknowing in the customs of your city,
Unus'd to the procedure of this court.
I beg you let me have some learnèd man
Of law an advocate to plead my cause.
Since I am forc'd to take a felon's place,
I would I might escape a felon's doom.
  Rigot. Inept! impertinent! and insolent!
The law allows not one who breaks the law,
When self-convicted, to defend his crime;
Nor might the keenest lawyer find a grain
Of innocence in all his chaff or words.
In sooth, he lies so well, no advocate
Could help him lie, or would affront the face
Of justice with his brazen impudence.
Let us proceed, at once proceed, to judgment.[16]
  [*Re-enter* POUPIN *and* BERNARD.
  Poupin. Why tarry ye, who are the ministers
Of justice! Do ye bear the sword in vain?
While ye sit here our pulpits call down vengeance:

The Reformer

Our solemn meetings are aflame with rage
And holy horror at this impious Spaniard.
Verily: if Satan had come out of hell,
He could not vomit forth worse blasphemies."
 Bernard. Ay—ay—he is an own son of the devil,
Well serv'd were he torn limb from limb."
 [*Shouts and groans outside.* Enter PERRIN *with* CITIZENS. *He takes his place as Chief Syndic.*"
 Perrin. We come to voice your judgment, noble
  lords;
Ye hear it in the shouts of the Two Hundred
And distant murmurs of the populace,
Demanding that this hapless stranger, cast
Within th' asylum of our open gates,
Have liberty,—with vengeance on the head
Of his pursuers. And so end the brawl,
Which mars the city's majesty and peace.
 Citizens. (*One after another.*) Liberty! Justice!
Vengeance! Down with Calvin!
 Servetus. Hear the Two Hundred: Down with
  Calvin!
 Berthelier. Vandel!
 Citizens.   Vandel! Vandel!
 Perrin.   Let Vandel speak!
 [HERALD *lifts his staff to signify silence.*
 Vandel. Ye come, my lord Chief Syndic, on the edge
Of time, as when a general arrives
To turn the battle from defeat and rout.
No hapless stranger is on trial now,
But free-born children of Geneva—you,
And I, and all of us, the whole republic—
At the behest of an intruding stranger,
As foreign to our laws as to our blood.
 [*Re-enter* CALVIN.

Citizens. The old French fox! Reynard! Reynard! Reynard!

Francesca. (*Appearing and disappearing in the crowd.*) Base, lying slanderer of my noble father!

Calvin. What crimes he hath committed ye well know
Who were his judges; and to veil such crimes
Is but to lose the veil of modesty,
In woman or in man.

Francesca. (*Reappearing and disappearing.*) Oh, ye soft hearts!
Weak judges cringing to a vagrant priest!
Must ev'n a woman shame you to be men?

Calvin. I pray you, let these brawlers know that they
Must go and build themselves another city
Ere they can make of yours their Babylon.

Francesca. You wicked man! you'd like to drink the blood
Of our family. But you will soon be driven
Out of Geneva!"

Servetus. Hunt him from your city, out!
Out like a blind man howling in a desert!
Brand him as with a red-hot cross of fire!
Wretch! Liar! Conjurer! Seducer! Tyrant!
Manslayer! Pity all your crimes,
As black and thick as swarming, stinging wasps,
Had not been nipp'd i' the belly of your mother!"

Citizens. Away with Calvin! Live Servetus!

D'Arlod. Shame!
Shame, senators! These tongues disgrace the ears
That hear them.

Perrin. Yet they voice the public will,
Albeit rudely. Have ye heard enough?
[*To the* HERALD.] Bid them away.

The Reformer

[*At the signal from* Perrin, *the* Herald, *bearing his staff before him, clears the hall and restores order.*

Calvin.   Let not the tumult move you, honored lords.
These idle charges waste themselves in air;
And with this obscene dog I bandy words
No more.   Ye now may see the mask torn off
The trait'rous faction here, that would drag down
Both Church and State into one common ruin.
  Vandel.   Who is this low-born Picard that dares talk
Of traitors among noble senators?
  Servetus.   Does he decree your doctrine like the Sorbonne?
  Perrin.   Have we no head?   No civic dignity?
Has this bold preacher-priest become confessor
To the whole city with his penances
And his inquisitorial court of morals?
Shall high-born nobles and patrician dames
Be driven from the altar of their sires
As excommunicate?   Must even a Favre
In chains cry "Liberty!" along our streets,
While the proud daughter of his ancient house
Lowers her coronet to prison bars,—
Because, forsooth, the pleasures of her rank
Suit not this carping censor of our manners
And this subverter of our cherish'd laws?
His yoke we cannot, and we will not bear.
  Calvin.   'T is not my yoke, most noble Syndic; nor
By me impos'd; it is the yoke of Christ
Ye would not bear;   And 'neath that yoke
The proudest their stiff necks shall bend; albeit
As many coronets as haughty heads
Were in the House of Favre!"
  Vandel.   Ho! ye gods!
Where is our Comic Cæsar now?   It seems

of Geneva.

There is a Hildebrand upon the stage,
With mock anathemas, like mimic thunders,
In his small theatre.
    Calvin.   A part I have
To act, upon a stage invisible
To mortal eyes, beneath th' all-seeing Judge,
With high onlooking angels round the scene
Where Truth with Error, Vice with Virtue strives,
While Christendom awaits th' unfolding plot
Of Providence. Be this my theatre:
With its applauses I shall be content,
Though all the world should smite me in the face.[25]
    D'Arlod. Bravo! A Cicero to Catiline!
    Berthelier. My lords, I have no hidden part to act;
Nor have I any sermon here to preach,
Such as we now have heard, and heard before,
But a plain matter of our law, too dull
And dry for pulpit-tricks or stage-effects,
Yet gravely real and of public weight.
Ye have arraign'd this learnèd foreigner,
A heretic, and if ye heed the words
Of his most rev'rend prosecutor——
    Servetus.   Tyrant!
Manslayer! Torturer!
    Berthelier.   Ye will at last
Condemn and burn him with anathemas.
Such power ye have in your high office; but
The power to punish carries power t' absolve[26];
And justice which ye mete to a mere stranger,
That justice must ye mete to one free-born,—
Ay, high-born, yet debarr'd our ancient altar.
Wherefore, I stand upon our civic rights
Against this new usurping court of aliens,
And claim your absolution from its censure,

The Reformer

With leave to take the Holy Eucharist,
Please God, on Sunday next.
    Vandel.   Vive Berthelier!
    Perrin.   Honor to his immortal sire!
    Senators.   Ay! Ay!
And freedom for us all!
    Calvin.   I pray you force me not, most honor'd lords,
To do what God forbids. In your own realm
Your will is mine. But one there is, the Lord
Of lords, our Master, whom I must obey,
Though I lay down my life.
    [CALVIN *stands aside in quiet dignity*.
    Poupin.   How dare we cast
The holy bread to dogs?
    Vandel.   A dog art thou
To speak so in this presence!
    Bernard.   Your new edicts
Yield to Christ's ministers His power of keys,
To open or to shut the gates of Heaven;
And being shut ye may not open them,
And let in outlaws to the Holy Feast.
    Perrin.   Talk not of new edicts. We have the old,
The rights episcopal as well as ducal.
The imperial eagle guards the Sacred Keys:"
    [*Pointing to the Arms of Geneva.*]
We dare not yield them into foreign hands.
Nor did we wrest them from the grasp of Rome
To put your petty popedom in its place.
    Servetus.   O worthy judges! Upright magistrates!
Well do ye bear your Christian dignities!
    Perrin.   Give to the noble Berthelier his warrant,
With the great seal. If minded to live well
And clear in his own conscience, he may take
The Holy Supper in our Church St. Peter,

of Geneva.

On Sunday next; and there attend we all
With him and see this mandate does not fail.
  [*The* SECRETARY *hands the document to* BERTHELIER.
  Servetus. Now justice, righteous lords, to one a stranger,
Yet mayhap heaven-sent deliverer.
Accuser of my accuser here I stand.
Bid to your bar as prisoner with me
This liar, persecutor, slanderer,
False teacher, this seducing Simon Magus,
This would-be murderer, John Calvin;
And by your *Lex talionis* take his life
For mine, with all his goods. No longer then
Can he bewitch and lord it o'er your city.
Lo! a Saint Michael come to slay the dragon!"
  [*Outcries of* " Hear! hear! " *and* " Shame! shame! "
  D'Arlod. My lords! my lords! we're like a wrangling crew
Upon a starless sea, and tempest-driven
We know not whither. What are these disputes,
These petty quarrels of inflam'd divines,
These ravings of a craz'd enthusiast
But mutiny in face of yawning shipwreck?
Or what our civic laws and precedents,
As weigh'd against the law and interest
Of Christendom? Look out beyond our walls.
Hath not even Rome made common cause with us
Against this prisoner? Send to Vienne,
That we may learn why they imprisoned him:
Why judg'd him guilty: and how he escaped.
And are we not confederate with the Swiss,
To stand or fall by our protector, Berne?
Let your State-Messenger go round the cantons
And from their syndics and their churches glean

The Reformer of Geneva.

Such counsel as shall make us of one mind.
Else rampant Anarchy will soon dissolve
Your Senate, and your streets run red with blood.
    Berthelier. (*Aside to his partisans.*) Appeal! appeal!
        Berne is no friend to Calvin,
And once pluck'd Bolsec from his logic vise.
    Vandel. The senator speaks wisely. We appeal——
    Servetus. To Berne! Let Berne be umpire!
    Perrin.   And what say
Our gracious lords the reverend ministers?
    Calvin. (*Aside to his Colleagues.*) Were we to say 't is
        daylight at high noon,
They would deny it in their present temper."[29]
    [*To* PERRIN.] Naught more, save that we join in the
        appeal—
From madness to sane reason—if found elsewhere.
Though earthly judges all prove weak and false,
There is a Judge of judges, sitting high
Above the passions of their erring state,
Who oft reverses their crude, hasty judgment
And turns their seeming wisdom into folly.
    Perrin. Well then! we seem to be at last agreed.
Nothing remains but that our embassies
Shall bring us further light and counsel. Meantime
Let Monsieur Calvin preach and do his duty.
So shall we hear the voice of Christendom,
And find out who is master in Geneva."[30]

ACT IV.

THE JUDGMENT OF CHRISTENDOM.

Scene   I.—A Room in the Captain-General's Palace.
Scene II.—A Dungeon in the Old Bishop's Palace.
Scene III.—The Senate Chamber in the Town-Hall.

ACT IV.

SCENE I.

A Room in the Palace of the CAPTAIN-GENERAL. *Enter* LA FONTAINE *and* IDELETTE.

   La Fontaine. At length the cloud has pass'd, the shadow gone,
And we are come into the light again,
Each dearer for the shadow and the cloud.
   Idelette. Since now thou art a true son of Geneva.
   La Fontaine. And thou, a daughter of the exiled Church.
So always in the clouded heaven of Love,
The stars are shining, though we see them not.
The faith of lovers, like their faith in God,
Is but refined by trials, and their hope
Shines like the moon through every passing sorrow.
   Idelette. Would that the skies would clear above this house!
Some murky trouble gathers over it.
I feel it in the air, as one can feel
The chill of coming storms. My moody father
Sits in unwonted silence; and, at times,
Unseen I hear my mother's angry tongue
Break out in fierce reproaches. Seldom now
They see me;—she, to watch me like a lynx,
And he, to only gaze with vacant look.

The Reformer

 La Fontaine. 'T is but a common madness of the hour
Which rages since that crack-brain'd heretic came
To turn the city upside-down.   Some plot,
I fear, is brewing elsewhere, if not here.
 Idelette. 'T was that so overcast my dreams last night.
I saw the city wake to Sabbath prayer
And praise.   The great bell, Clémence, peal'd o'er town
And lake and distant vale.   The streets were throng'd
With worshippers; and in the temples choirs
Of children sang their practic'd melodies,
The songs of our sweet psalmodist, Marot.'
And then I saw wild bands of dark-brow'd men,
With murd'rous looks and daggers drawn.   And then—
I shudder but to think of what I saw.
 La Fontaine.   A dream, yet not a dream.   Often our dreams
Are only dreams.   Th' unguarded thoughts in sleep,
When freed from Reason and the regnant Will,
Are but mere lawless images of things
By Fancy led as in a masque and revel,
Yet sometimes show the habit of the mind
And its affinity with good or evil.
Then wicked souls, like puppets grossly mov'd,
Make sport for mocking demons; but the good,
Whose waking thoughts are pure, ev'n in their dreams
Lie open to all heavenly influence
And gracious ministry of kindred spirits.
The dear remember'd dead come back to them.
Angels may visit them in troublous times
With warning visions of impending woes;
And they in turn become like angels, who
Can see us better than we see ourselves,
And guard us from the ills to which we 're prone.

of Geneva.

Perhaps thy dream thou wilt remember, should
Its pictur'd terrors come in sight, and then
Of some safe refuge think for those still dear,
Some hiding-place beyond the city walls.
Meanwhile, fear not, but trust in Heaven's grace
Which yet may bring ev'n to this troubl'd House,
As to Geneva, " after darkness light."
    [*Exeunt* LA FONTAINE *and* IDELETTE.

 [*Enter* PERRIN *and* BERTHELIER.
 Berthelier. 'T is time for " Cæsar " to be tragical.
 Perrin. Methinks we 've had enough of comedy.
 Berthelier. Too much. This madcap Spaniard mars
  the plot.
The senators will have no more of him.
The cantons will adjudge him to the stake.
'T will but remain to lift him as a martyr
Before an angry, surging populace,
And whelm our foes as in a storm of blood.
Then may he serve us better dead than living.
 Perrin. I hope we yet may save as well as use him.
 Berthelier. I much fear it. Our pious tyrant prayed
As if he were prime-minister of Heaven,
And doubtless sent before our Messenger
Letters to shape the judgment he invok'd.
So do such saints oft answer their own prayers.
And now we can but thwart his art with force,
That desp'rate remedy for tyranny
No less than heresy.
 [*Goes to the door and admits* GUEROULT.]
     Here is Gueroult,
Come to report as to your secret orders.
 Gueroult. I have obeyed them as a willing slave.

The Reformer

Perrin.   Are the men listed?
Gueroult.   Ay, and posted all
By fifties in the sev'ral parishes,
Like prowling wolves among the sleeping folds.
   Perrin.   And armed?
   Gueroult.   Well armed: [*Draws his
      dagger, and throws open his cloak, to show a white
      cross on his doublet.*]
                        Each with a figured doublet,
Designed to flatter the Consistory
And help the Lord to know His own.
   Perrin.   Gueroult,
You jest too much.   This is most serious.
   Gueroult.   And I am serious.   Revenge but seems
To make men merry.
   Perrin.   Go with him, Berthelier:
See all the captains, charge them each by oath
To answer any gen'ral call to arms.
And let the Great Bell give the signal peal.
            [*Exeunt* BERTHELIER *and* GUEROULT.

   [*Enter* IDELETTE, *kneeling before* PERRIN.
   Idelette.   O my good father, I like not the faces
Of those two men:—have nought to do with them—
I saw them pass—have seen them in my dreams,
Wearing white crosses all besmeared with blood,
And rushing among slaughter'd men and babes
And women who stretch'd out their hands to Heaven——
   Perrin.   Poor child! thy weak young nerves are all
         unstrung,   [*lifting her up*]
Come to thy mother.
   Idelette.   No! no! tell her not,
Flee, flee with her out of this doomèd city,

of Geneva.

Beyond the wall—t' our country-seat—until
The storm is past!

[*Exit* IDELETTE, *as* FRANCESCA *enters from the opposite side.*

Francesca. Is all arranged?
Perrin. (*Absently.*)   All is arranged.
Francesca.   Gueroult
And Berthelier have both been here?
Perrin. (*Absently.*)   Gueroult
And Berthelier have both been here.
Francesca. What means this absent mood? This pallor on
A cheek that never blanches? Art thou sick?
Perrin. Sick? Sick of the whole bloody business! I
Have had a warning as from heaven.
Francesca.   Tut! Tut!
Womanish fancies, mere dyspeptic humors,
Bred of last night's debauch, as the brain cools,
And turns its images to horrid shapes.
Shake off these visions of a morbid creed,
Be no weak Herod to this would-be John
The Baptist. Make not me a Herod's wife
To dare thee bring his head upon a charger!
Perrin. (*Still absently looking where* IDELETTE *had vanished.*)
What if this were an angel voice?
Francesca.   Aha!
My lord is in his rôle of " Tragic Cæsar."
If this mood lasts, I'll play the Amazon
To muster forth his troop of fierce crusaders
And through the streets cry out " To arms! to arms!"
                              [*Withdrawing.*
Perrin. (*Recovering.*) " To arms!" I should be ready for that call,

The Reformer

Who never yet did hear it but to heed it!
And I must follow it, though it lead me on
Through seas of carnage to the brink of hell.
    [*Exit* PERRIN, *following* FRANCESCA.

SCENE II.

A Dungeon in the Old Bishop's Palace. SERVETUS *appears, wasted and in ragged clothes.*[2]

Servetus. Day after day—week after week—and still
No tidings from the cantons. Morn and eve,
The prison lights and shadows come and go
Only to mock my hopes,—and I grow sick
At heart and wasted with this foul disease,
This darkness, silence, and oblivion.
O my good Christian masters, Turks would treat
Me less unkindly! and you summer friends,
Where are ye now? Yet I live on, and dream
Of liberty, as starving men will dream
Of feasts. [*Goes to the window and looks out.*]
   So pined afar in Chillon's walls
That other prisoner of tyranny,
The patriot Bonnivard, through six long years,
Immured below the ripples of the lake
Until his island-dungeon seem'd a tomb.
Then came deliverers and burst the bars,
As in a miracle of resurrection,
And led him forth into the living world
To free the State—as I would free the Church.
 [*Clanging doors are opened behind him and light streams into the prison as* CLAUDE *enters.*]

Ha! is the vision real? while I dream'd it!
Light! Freedom! Glory! have ye come at last?
   Claude. Be ready for the worst!
   Servetus.   The worst! I dream'd
It was the best.
   Claude.   The cantons with one voice
Decree the penalty of heresy.
   Servetus. O God! it must not be! It is too terrible.
To die—to die accursed. I cannot bear it.
O misery! Mercy! Mercy! Mercy! [*Falls into a
    paroxysm.*
   Claude. Poor wretch! Thou canst not play the
    Christian: be
At least a man.
   Servetus.   'T is harder here to play
The Christian than the man.
   Claude.   Take one more hope:
Know that Gueroult, made desp'rate by the news,
Is mustering now his bands. Thanks to their courage—
Not to thy faith—thou mayest yet be free.
   Servetus. Bear with me, Claude. Thou 'rt no anato-
    mist,
And hast not pried into this curious frame
To see what vexing tricks it plays with us,
When under sudden impulse from the brain,
The nimble blood is scar'd into the heart,
Like troops recoiling to a citadel,
Thence to rush out again and reinforce
The coward nerves and the o'ermastered will.³
I 'm better now.
   Claude.   And I must go. New guards
And stricter take my place.⁴   [*Exit* CLAUDE.
   [*Enter Guards with* FAREL, *followed by two* SYNDICS
    and CALVIN.⁵

The Reformer

Servetus.   Ugh! there 's that Farel,
Who always stirs the hidden devil in me:
So lion-hearted, yet so meek he seems.
Now pluck up thy whole self, a true Saint Michael,
To fight these dragons in their guise of saints.
Why have ye come hither?
    Farel.   To save thy soul.
    Servetus. Thou 'rt not its Saviour.
    Farel.   And the souls of those
Thou seekest to destroy with heresy.
Recant, that life may come to thee and them,
And peace be made 'twixt brethren in the Church.
    Servetus. What ye call heresy I call the truth.
Can I recant the truth? and ye alone
Make brethren fight. How then can I make peace?
    Farel. Thou hast the sacred name of Christ dis-
      honor'd.
    Servetus. Proof! Cite one text for an eternal Christ!
    Farel. In principio erat Verbum; ——
    Servetus.   Tush!
Old straw thrice thresh'd. Let 's have no more of that.
    A Syndic. Have mercy on thyself. We ministers
Of Justice even would be merciful
And pluck thee as a brand from out the flames.
    Servetus. Away, ye cruel tempters! ye may kill
The body but ye cannot kill the soul;
And though ye cast my books into the fires
Of hell, their thoughts shall smoulder in the minds
Of men, and some day set the world aflame.
Begone! Mockers and murderers are ye all.
    Syndic. Die if thou wilt. Yet make thy peace with
      him
Thou hast so wrong'd.
    Servetus.   Calvin? Him I would see.

Calvin. (*Coming forward.*) What would'st thou have?
Servetus.   Thy pardon, as we part.
Calvin. 'T was given ere 't was ask'd. No petty spite
Have I pursued through all this war of words.
None could I drag into this last, stern hour.
Remember how we met in youth at Paris;
Even then, and at the risk of life, I sought
To curb thy daring flight; and since that time
Have pray'd good men might take thee by the hand
And lead thee to the way of truth; and thou
Hast shower'd after me, I know not what—
Scarce sane it seemed. Let all that be forgotten.
Ask pardon but of Him thy Saviour, whom
Thou hast degraded from the throne of Heaven,
And seek His mercy ere it be too late.
   [SERVETUS *falls into a reverie. The others withdraw.*
Farel. Ah! if he only would recant!
Syndic.   No! no!
We cannot spare him now.
Calvin.   Is it not written:
" An heretic that hath been twice reproved
Ye shall reject, as one who but condemns
Himself " ?   [*Exeunt.*
   [SERVETUS *remains in reverie. Re-enter Guards with*
      TISSOT *and the* SECRETARY OF JUSTICE.
Tissot. (*Aside.*) So chang'd! What spiritual Power
Restores his reason ? [*Touching his shoulder.*]
                Come with me
To hear of the good pleasure of my Lords.
Servetus. I follow, like my Master, but to die.'
                [*Exeunt.*

The Reformer

SCENE III.

The Senate Chamber in the Town-Hall. D'ARLOD *is pacing meditatively. Enter to him* COLLADON.

Colladon.   I find thee where the State has need of thee,
Lord Syndic; but the Senate still not here!
What stays the sentence of the heretic?
  D'Arlod.   They say our doughty Captain has a headache.
  Colladon.   Ah! to be sure!   Or call it stomach-ache:
Say he hath eaten unripe fruit, and now
His ill-digested scheme agrees not with him,
As one by one the cantons range themselves
Against his protégé.
  D'Arlod.   Poor maniac!
What shall be done with him, much troubles us.
This morning we must hear the embassies
That will conclude his guilt: And then—What then?
We may not turn him loose in Christendom,
A wolf to worry the whole flock of Christ;
Nor dare we keep him pent up in Geneva
As a mere smother'd brand of revolution—
Do with him what we will, he is a plague
Upon the State.   We never shall have peace
'Till we are rid of him.
  Colladon.   Ay, ay: to this
The brethren say Amen.   It hath become
The general verdict, ever since the day
When Berthelier, that graceless reprobate,
Was smitten by the secret wrath of God.
So dread and awful was the scene, while round
The holy table came his impious crew—
Foul harpies fain to snatch the heavenly food,—

And like another holy Chrysostom,
Fearless our great Reformer stood and cried,
With hands extended o'er the elements;—
"Away! Profane! Ye would but eat and drink
Damnation to yourselves. Cut off these hands,
Ere they shall give the sacred things of God
To those whom He hath branded His despisers!"
Back through the parting throng the apostate fled
As though a flaming sword had driven him forth;
And fear fell on the saints, and brooding awe,
While silently they took the bread and wine.⁷
And now there is a dread of pending judgments,
Because that heretic Servetus lives
An Achan in the camp. Saith not the Law
As writ in Deuteronomy Thirteenth
"A false prophet ye shall surely put to death." ⁸
   D'Arlod. Thou art a churchly statesman, Colladon,
And readest earthly things in heavenly light,
By visions and portents of Holy Writ.
But wordly conflicts call for arts and arms
As well as prayers. These plotting libertines,
Be sure, withdrew with some dark policy;
And even amid the general awe which reigns
Are lurking now like vermin in the shade.
   [*Enter* LA FONTAINE *hurriedly.*
   La Fontaine. My duty to you, gentlemen, in haste.
I must be brief. The dastard plot is all
Unveil'd. Our wily Berthelier himself,
As overheard when garrulous in his cups,⁹
Has dropt the pass-word, sign, and countersign;
And telltale parcels of white crosses show
Where Claude and Gueroult have their secret haunts.
The lying butcher-signal may be flouted
At any moment in our streets. I wait

The Reformer

Your orders, losing time.
 D'Arlod. (*To* Colladon.) How many names
Of citizens, said'st thou, were registered?
 Colladon. At least three hundred, the best blood of
  France.
 D'Arlod. (*To* La Fontaine.) Go have them arm'd,
  and by that well-won sword
Of thine, win back new freedom for Geneva.
        [*Exit* La Fontaine.
 Colladon. This is a sov'reign remedy for headache.
 D'Arlod. Ay, it will kill or cure. [*Voices outside.*]
       Now comes the Senate,
With a quick sentence to the heretic.

[*Enter the* Senate *of* Twenty-Five, *preceded by the* City Herald *and the escort of Archers*. Perrin *presides; on one side* Berthelier, Vandel, *and three other Conspirators; on the other side*, D'Arlod, Du Pan, Calvin, *and three other Colleagues. The French* Papal Envoy *and Attendants with a Jailer and the Swiss* State-Messenger *are in waiting*.
 Perrin. I have been ill, most noble lords, more ill
In mind than body, with a boding sense
Of evils coming on the State, which yet
I trust our wisdom somehow may avert.[10]
We wait the embassies. First, from Vienne.
 Herald. (*Ushering the French* Papal Envoy *and Jailer.*)
The sage, illustrious, and magnificent
Lords of Vienne, by this their honor'd envoy!
 Perrin. What say your noble masters should be done
As to our prisoner, Michael Servetus?
 Envoy. With all due courteous greeting, simply this:

of Geneva.

Your prisoner, Servetus, at Vienne,
Known as Villeneuve, hath been already tried,
Condemn'd, and even burn'd in effigy,
Together with the five bales of his book.
Wherefore we pray you to remand him hence
Unto our court in Dauphiny, and let
This jailer take his body there and make
That real which were else a futile show
Of justice, and mere mockery of law.
So may you spare yourselves much further trouble.
    Perrin. A point of law for you, most learned Rigot.
    Rigot. The prisoner himself should make election
To go or stay; but if he own our laws,
We cannot give him up and must ourselves
See justice done.
    Perrin.   He shall be brought before us,
And make his choice.
    Envoy.   But should he choose to stay
And own your laws, we then some written proof
Must have from him that by no fault of ours,
No aid or favor, he broke jail and brought
Such scandal on our Holy Inquisition.
    Perrin. Whatever he confesses ye shall have
With his sign-manual.
    Envoy.   And furthermore:
His goods, some thousand crowns and more,
Are now confiscate; and our King of France
By his lieutenant here demands to know
The debts and credits due on the estate.
    Perrin. A gracious answer make, and say from us,
Full justice by our edicts shall be done
Alike upon his body and his goods.
    Envoy. This seems all fair. If we must leave him
        here,

The Reformer

Thank God we leave him in good hands, with those
Who will not let him slip again, nor fail
In zeal against a common enemy.
Meanwhile we wait his choice and your good pleasure."
      [*Exeunt* ENVOY *and attendants. Manet Failer.*
  Perrin. Now let us hear the cities of the Swiss.
  Herald. (*Ushering the* STATE-MESSENGER.)
The noble lords of Berne, Schaffhausen, Zurich,
And Basel, by this trusty Messenger!
  Perrin. The purport of these messages we know:
Give but the pith of them, and waste no words.
  Messenger. (*Glancing through each roll as he reads.*)
Our potent ally BERNE condemns Servetus
As a destroyer of the Christian faith;
Is much incensed by all his arrogance;
And prays we may have strength to put the churches
At once beyond the reach of such a pest.
      BASEL has grown intolerant for once
And counsels, if he cannot be reclaim'd,
To use the utmost power of our office
That we may stop his troubling of the Church.
      ZURICH, so moderate, is deeply griev'd
At the impunity of heretics,
And begs us make of him a lesson, which
Shall wipe off the reproach in time to come.
      And blunt SCHAFFHAUSEN calls his blasphemy
A wasting gangrene in the limbs of Christ,
And warns us that to reason with him more,
Would but be growing crazy with a fool.
      All leave to us the choice of penalty;
But Berne, we know by mandatory hint,
Would have us cast him to the flames.
That Heaven so may guide you, is their prayer.
            [*Exit the* STATE-MESSENGER.

of Geneva.

Perrin.   A dismal showing this.
D'Arlod.   He is adjudg'd
Guilty in the high court of Christendom;
By Protestant as well as Catholic.
   Calvin.   (*Withdrawing with his Colleagues.*)
Bear witness, honor'd lords, we have not urg'd
Nor stayed this general judgment; and we now
Must leave with you alone the penalty.
The tongue and pen are ours, and not the sword,
To prove, but not to punish heresy:
That we account your sole prerogative,
As heaven-sent guardians of our earthly peace,
For us ordained of God the Powers that be.
And since the State must keep its course of justice,
The Church can only plead with you for mercy."
If in your wisdom ye a forfeit life
Can save and save the State which it doth put
In peril, then let mercy turn the scale;
The which God grant.—But since ye judge not so,
We pray you spare th' atrocity of fire,
And use instead the quick and painless sword.
Leave to our foes their mock *auto-da-fé*
And let not scoffers weave its cruel flames
A martyr halo through all coming time.
                  [*Exeunt* CALVIN *with his Colleagues.*
   Perrin.   Mercy! Who dares to plead for mercy what
Is due to justice and to innocence?
Shall meddling parsons shape our civic rule?
And foreign voices drown our native sense
Of right? Be just, and so be merciful,
To one, who though of alien creed, is still
The city's guest; and let the city's voice
Be heard for him, where only it can speak;—
Not here, but in the Council of Two Hundred!

The Reformer

D'Arlod.   Treason!
Du Pan.   Treason!
[*Outcries of* " The Plot!" " The Plot!"   *Groans and hisses.*
Perrin. (*Leaving the Chair.*)
Enough! enough!   I will not be your Pilate,
To wash from hypocritic hands the blood
Ye mean to shed.   [*Withdrawing with Conspirators.*]
We go from these mad counsels;
Honor flees where Justice cannot stay;
Now light up, if ye will, that funeral pyre
Where future Genevese shall come to weep and wish
That they might quench it with their tears.
        [*Exeunt* PERRIN *and the Conspirators.*
D'Arlod.   Now Law and Order may resume their sway,
Since Treason and Misrule have gone elsewhere,
To plot that mischief which they dare not here,
And which we now must thwart with swifter doom
Upon their tool and would-be leader.   Justice?
Our word is plighted to Vienne and Berne
That fullest justice shall be done.   Mercy?
No mercy can be shown to one who shows
No mercy to himself.   A second time
He rushes to the flames.   With his own hand
Plucks down the highest penalty of law—
Do not our edicts call for death by fire?
   Senators.   Ay!   Ay!
   D'Arlod.   Let him be brought to judgment."
[*Ushered by the* HERALD *and Guards enter* TISSOT, *the* SECRETARY OF JUSTICE, FAREL, *and* SERVETUS.
   D'Arlod.   Michael Servetus, alias Villeneuve,
By which of these two names wilt thou be called?
Choose whether to go with this jailer to Vienne,

Or here await thy sentence? [*The Jailer approaches.*

    Servetus. (*Kneeling before the Judges.*) Cast me not,
Most merciful lords, into the flames I have
Escap'd. Let me in thy good pleasure hope,
Whate'er it be.

    D'Arlod. Then art thou twice condemn'd.
Syndics and Senators, as here conjoined
In the tribunal of your ancestors,
Having before your eyes the Holy Scriptures,
The canons of the code Justinian,
The civic edicts and the embassies,
The evidence as to this prisoner
How judge ye——?

    Syndics. Let him be anathema.

    Senators. Anathema.

    D'Arlod. Break over him the staff
Of honor.

    Tissot. (*Breaking a staff above his head.*) Anathema.

    D'Arlod. Michael Servetus,
Guilty of heresy, of blasphemy,
And of disturbing Christendom,
Thou art condemn'd to be led to the place
Of Champel; to be bound there to a stake;
And with thy books and writings in thy girdle,
To be then burn'd alive, until thy body
Has been reduced to ashes. So thy days
Shall end in warning to all like offenders.

    Servetus. The sword in mercy! and not fire! lest I
Despair and lose my soul! [*Falling prostrate.*

    Du Pan. Too late! too late!
Another voice has prayed that prayer in vain!

    Farel. (*Lifting up* SERVETUS.) Confess thy crime!

    Servetus. I have not sinn'd——

    Farel. Repent! else I must leave thee to thy fate.

The Reformer of Geneva.

Servetus. Or if I sinn'd, I sinn'd in ignorance.
Farel. Hear, gracious lords! have pity! pardon him!
D'Arlod. Guards! do your duty.
[SERVETUS *and* FAREL *are quickly surrounded with the escort of Archers and preceded by the* HERALD *and* LORD LIEUTENANT. [*Exeunt.*
Servetus. (*Exclaiming as he disappears.*)
Son of the Eternal God, have mercy on me!"

ACT V.

THE TRIUMPH OF THE REFORMATION.

Scene   I.—The Public Square and Town-Hall.
Scene II.—Before the Cathedral.
Scene III.—The Interior of the Cathedral.

ACT V.

SCENE I.

The Public Square. Steps leading up to the Town-Hall. The Rhone and Alps in view. A group of Sailors, Peasants, and Artisans standing idly about.

  First Bystander. Another boat-load of the French
    out yonder!
  Second Bystander. Ay, and that means more work-
    men on our walls
And on our quays and streets.
  First Bystander.   It means starvation.
The devil take these Frenchmen! They pull down
Our wages and put up the price of bread.
  Second Bystander. But bring the Gospel to us!
  First Bystander.   I like not
That new imported article; it is
Too green; 't will breed a deadly cholic in
The belly of the State. The renegades
Come running here so fast, the wafer still
Sticks in their throats.
  Second Bystander.   They promise us
New Freedom!
  First Bystander. Bah! We were free to go
To mass: now we are forc'd to go to sermon,
Or pay three sous.[1] We sit and hear ourselves

The Reformer

Berated in long prayers, and have our nerves
Fil'd into shreds with donkey-braying psalms.[2]
                    [*Gives a nasal imitation.*
  Second Bystander. Hush! hush! you will be fin'd or
    jail'd for this.
  CALVIN, *with a tome under his arm, passes gravely along,
    followed by* CLAUDE *and* GUEROULT, *hooting at him
    until he disappears:*
  Dog! Tyrant! Pope Calvin! To the Rhone with
    him!
  [*The group approach* CLAUDE *and* GUEROULT.
  First Bystander. Ho! What now?
  Gueroult.   Vengeance!
  Claude. 'T was but a cruel murder.
  Second Bystander.   Where? When?
  Claude. Have ye not heard the news,—the heretic
That has been foully burned alive at Champel?[3]
  First Bystander. Pooh! that 's not new, but common:
    anyone
Must burn that will not keep a canting tongue.
  Second Bystander. Was he a Catholic or Protestant?
  Claude. Neither. He said that both were wrong,
    and he
Had come to set them right.
  Second Bystander.   And which was right?
  Claude. Well, they both burn'd him and that settl'd it.
  Second Bystander. But which was right?
  Claude. (*To* GUEROULT.) Say which was orthodox.
  Gueroult. The Lord only knows. These reverend
    doctors have
As many orthodoxies as bald pates.
They reason with a heretic before
They roast him, as a cat plays with a mouse,—
To give him seeming chances for his life;

of Geneva.

And in their Latin billingsgate will call
Each other *canis, mendax, nebulo,*
As glibly as we say " dog," " liar," " rascal."
But when the word-fight has its gala-day,
And book and heretic must blaze together—
Mark you! the noble syndics understand
Neither the book nor who 's the heretic.
This time they flay'd a simple wand'ring scholar.
   Second Bystander. Did he die game?
   Gueroult. I hear, like any other holy martyr.
   [*Enter* BERTHELIER.] Lord Berthelier,
Some listeners as to the late martyrdom.
   First Bystander. Come and let us hear this fine gentleman.
   [*They gather around him.*
   Berthelier. O never did the sun on such a sight
Look down, eclips'd at noon with smoke and glare,
Sent up as from the flaming mouth of hell
Into the face of heaven. 'T would make you grind
Your teeth and weep with rage, were I to paint
The human devils in that scene.*
   Gueroult.   Death to 'em!
   Berthelier. But not of them I speak, to waste your tears;—
Only of that poor victim of their hate.
'T was pitiful to see him chain'd and bound,
The green wood stack'd about his trembling limbs;
A sulphurous wreath of oak-leaves on his head,
And at his girdle tied the foolish books
They call'd heretical.
   Claude.   Shame! Shame!
   Gueroult.   Revenge!
   Berthelier. Then came the murderous torch — the blazing chaplet—

The Reformer

The crackling fagots and the lurid flames,
Stifling his piteous prayers.
   Bystanders.   Horrible!
   Berthelier. Alas! no priestly hand with crucifix
Before his dying eye—but all the while
The mocking preachments [FAREL *appears*] of yon canting zealot!
   All. Farel! Farel! To the Rhone with him! To the Rhone!
   [*As they rush toward* FAREL, *an arquebus is fired off by* GUEROULT, *exploding at the trigger.*
   Farel. (*Snapping his fingers at them.*)
Cowards! Would ye kill the servants of the Most High?
   [*At the same moment he is surrounded by the Ministers, led by* LA FONTAINE *with drawn sword.*
   La Fontaine. Back! By the armed majesty of law!
   [*Following* LA FONTAINE, *enter the armed Refugees forming a guard around* FAREL *and the Ministers, while* D'ARLOD *and the* SENATORS *group themselves near the steps of the Town-Hall. On the other side where the other group have retreated, Francesca rushes in and out excitedly.*
   Francesca. The French! the French! they're going to sack the city!
To arms! to arms!
   Berthelier. (*Rushing out with* FRANCESCA.) To arms! good citizens!

   [*Enter* IDELETTE *to* LA FONTAINE.
   Idelette. Our Master comes! I've read it in his face!
   La Fontaine. Not now! not here! into the jaws of death!
Go, save thyself and him!

of Geneva.

Farel. Bid him not come!
Idelette. He would not heed me, but mov'd sternly on,
Smiling as with a dying benediction.
He comes with such a look as martyrs wear.
La Fontaine. Alas! back to thy prayers!
Idelette. (*Appealing to Heaven.*) Oh, save him! save him!
And save Geneva! [*Exit.*

[*The Great Bell is pealing rapidly. Re-enter* BERTHE-
LIER, *with* PERRIN, VANDEL, *and the band of Con-
spirators, wearing white crosses and shouting
"Liberty! Liberty!"*
Vandel. (*While forming the ranks behind* PERRIN.)
Down with La Fontaine, Farel, Calvin, all!
Kill every French rascal that shows his head!
Perrin. (*Seizing from* D'ARLOD *the* SYNDIC'S *bâton
and waving it before the rioters.*)
The bâton must not pass to alien hands!
We rescue it from those not fit to bear it,
And hold it as our pledge of victory.
Forward! for the honor of Geneva!
La Fontaine. Stand in defence of Christ and of His Church!
[*Swords are drawn on both sides.*
[CALVIN *now appears in the background with folded arms
amid cries of* "Kill him!" "Death to him!" *from
the Conspirators. Looking them fixedly in the face,
and advancing between the ranks, he stoops upon one
knee, throws open his mantle, and bares his breast.*
Calvin. If ye want blood, here are some drops to shed.
Before heaven I come to offer up myself

The Reformer

A sacrifice.   Ye will not strike?   Then hear me!
   [*Rising he goes to the Town-Hall steps.*]
Ye children of Geneva! and ye sons of France!
Let reason stay awhile your swords in truce,
If so ye yet may sheathe them without blood.
   [*The swords are lowered.*]
Twice have ye called me to your city, still
So beautiful in hope, so rich in memory,—
But why so rent with feud and stain'd with sin?
Am I become the enemy of your peace?
Speak but the word, I go at once, and leave
In other hands the reins ye put in mine.
   [*Pointing first to Conspirators, and then to Refugees.*]
Behold on that side Treason, License, Crime,
And bloody Anarchy; on this behold
Religion, Virtue, Liberty, and Law;
And let your Senate choose between.
   [CALVIN *takes* D'ARLOD'S *arm and is followed by the* SENATORS *into the Town-Hall, while the combatants on both sides sheathe their swords, the Conspirators sullenly retiring, and the Refugees embracing one another for joy.*'

SCENE II.

Before the Gothic Doorway of the Cathedral.

   [*Enter* BERNARD *and* POUPIN, *approaching the Church door.*
   Bernard.   Now Korah, Dathan, and Abiram shall
Be swallowed up with all their rebel crew.
The judgment of the Senate will be swift
To my lords Perrin, Berthelier, and Vandel!

Poupin. Ay, for their sins this people long have
  suffer'd.
As Israel danc'd even at the foot of Sinai,
They have been steep'd in godless revelry.
But lo! our Moses, shining from the Mount,
Renews the broken tables of the Law.
  [*Entering the Church.*]
'T is well to give ourselves to prayer and praise—
And then go we to the Consistory.
  [*At the same time* CALVIN *enters pensively and follows
  them into the Cathedral, a Choir of children inside
  singing.**
Choir. Hail! My Redeemer! Sacrifice
    For all my guilt and pain and woe!
  What thanks, what praises will suffice,
    When to Thine altar I shall go?
  Ah! nothing thither can I bring,
    To tell of what to me Thou art;
  No other gift or offering
    Than this poor flaming, melting heart.

  [*Enter two* CITIZENS, *meeting.*
First Citizen. Whither so fast, good friend?
Second Citizen. (*Hurrying by.*) To the Town-Hall.
First Citizen. Come back, and save your steps.
Second Citizen. (*Returning.*) Can I, in sooth?
What has been done with the conspirators?
First Citizen. Oh, a quick end was made of them!
    Gueroult
And Claude, even where they stood resisting law,
Were slain with their own butcher swords,
And their white crosses made all red with blood.
Vandel is to be hang'd and drawn and quarter'd.

The Reformer

Second Citizen.   And my lord Berthelier——
First Citizen.   Will lose his head;
Yet out of feeling to his patriot sire
Is to have decent burial by his side.
  Second Citizen.   And what of our poor Captain-
    general?
  First Citizen.   Ah! there the Senate paus'd awhile.
    He had
Been Calvin's friend, and after his first fall
Calvin had plead for him and even to
The Holy Sacrament had welcom'd him.
So much weak treach'ry could no more be trusted.
He is to have an honorable death.
But his right hand, cut off and clasp'd around
The syndic's bâton, which he wav'd when he
Led on the rioters, is to be nail'd
Above his empty senate-chair, a warning
To all such traitors."
  Second Citizen.   When will all this be?
  First Citizen.   That's not yet certain.   Both of them
    are missing.
Since Madame Perrin fled to her country-seat.
I think they're also there, or will be soon.
                              [*Exeunt* CITIZENS.

[*Enter* BERTHELIER *leading* PERRIN.
  Berthelier.   Quick!   This way!
  Perrin.   Stay!   But one brief look across
The city walls at yonder river, lake,
And mountain.
  Berthelier.   Tush! we'll have a longer look,
And safer, when outside the city walls.
And Madame Perrin waits.   [*Pulls him towards the exit.*

of Geneva.

Perrin. O Francesca!
The play-house Cæsar is play'd out! [*Exeunt.*

[*Enter* LA FONTAINE, *meeting* IDELETTE, *emerging from the Cathedral door.*
Idelette. A happy eve!
La Fontaine. A happier morrow morn!
All heavenly portents come like wedding-guests
To greet our wedding-day.
  Idelette. And good men's prayers.
  [*They walk to and fro.*]
But now, I knelt where first I plighted faith
With love. Thither from the Consistory
Our Master came; and after grave advice
And blessing, his worn spiritual face
Grew strangely young again. He had divin'd
Our secret from the first, he said; and spoke
So sweetly of thy nobleness and truth.
And then, I know not why it was—as if
He crav'd some sympathy, he pour'd out all
His own strange history; presag'd to be
A life of sorrow and of strife even when
As a child crucifier he bore to mass
A heavy cross-hilt ending in a sword.[10]
Torn a shy student from his books, and sent
Against his will, as by a Higher Will
Which yet he made his own, he found himself
In scenes of violence and crime; weigh'd down
With mighty tasks; consum'd with cares of State
And Church abroad; bereft of wife and child
At home; fretted alike by friends and foes;
And badgerèd by sland'rous tongues. And so,
Save for the few who knew that glowing heart,

The Reformer

He cas'd it with a breastplate wrought of steel,
And made some think him cruel who was kind.
Now I no longer fear but pity him.
How must his wife have lov'd him! Oftentimes
We women worship a stern power in men
That makes more strange and sweet their tenderness,
Like flow'rets hid beneath the Alpine crags.

SCENE III.

Interior of the Cathedral of St. Peter. Trumpets outside and joy-bells from the church tower. Enter the CITY HERALD, *Ushers, Civic officers, Nobles, and Dames,* CITIZENS, *Burghers, Peasants, Artisans. To a dais,* D'ARLOD *with the Senate on one side, and on the other* CALVIN *with the Consistory.*

D'Arlod. Since Treason, License, Anarchy, and Crime
Are slain, or fled beyond the city gates,
Religion, Virtue, Liberty, and Law
Have come to grace this glad and solemn day.
'T is meet to welcome them with so much joy.
Give them our homage and sworn fealty,
As our Lord Secretary reads the oath.
  [*The* STATE SECRETARY *reads, all standing.*]
" We Syndics, Senators, Pastors, Doctors,
" Nobles, and commons of all sorts, assembl'd
" At sound of trumpet and the great church bell,
" And with our hands uplift to the Most High, [*all hands lifted*]
" Do swear allegiance to the Church Reform'd,

of Geneva.

"In name of Father, Son, and Holy Ghost."
[*A Gloria is sung by the Choir of Children in the bridal train of* IDELETTE *and* LA FONTAINE.

D'Arlod. So "AFTER DARKNESS LIGHT." Be it perpetual.

Calvin. Behold the victory of Christ! He rides
As in a flaming chariot on the winds,
And tramples down all Error, Vice, and Sin!
The spiritual conqueror of the world!
Crown him, ye poets, with the laurel-wreath;
And let the generations yet to come
Sing *Io Pæan* to the King of kings!"

Farel. Behold also God's chosen instrument,
Our Moses leading through the wilderness,
And the law-giver of our Israel!

Calvin. Mingle no praise of man with this high work
Of God. Remember, Israel's law-giver,
Because he smote the rock of Meriba
In sinful anger, could not enter Canaan,
But only viewed it from far Pisgah's top
And died unhonor'd with a sepulchre.
So have ye seen like vehemence untam'd[12]
In him ye call the leader of your cause.
For this he craves forgiveness of you all,
In sight of God, of angels, and of men.
Millions for this may call him tyrant, who
Shall owe to him their liberty; and though
All Christian lands should be his monument,
Let no man know his grave.[13]
                        The glory is
Not ours.—We are but shadows that o'ercloud it—
This living scene, and all that it portends,
The earth and sky around us, with the pomps

The Reformer of Geneva.

Of rising morn and sinking eve, are but
The pageantry of one Creative Mind,
Upheld and mov'd by one Eternal Will—
The glory give to One alone!

> [*Overcome by the vision he sinks down as in a swoon. The* SENATORS *and* PASTORS *gather around him, while* FAREL *supports his head.*

Tissot.   Stand back!   More light! more light!
Farel.   What need of it?
He hath such light as this world knows not of.
The glory of the Lord hath smitten him—
That glory which no man can see and live!
And now, like dying Simeon, he departs
In happy vision.

   D'Arlod.   And in charity
With all the world.   Ev'n as he sought forgiveness,
So let him be forgiven.

> [LA FONTAINE *and* IDELETTE *kneel at his feet.*

Idelette.   Who can tell
But that his spirit lingers near us still
With some last word of blessing?

   Calvin. (*Reviving for the moment.*)   Blessed! blessed!
As in the bridal of the Church with her
Own Heavenly Lord!   (*With hands joined as in devotion, he dies.*)

   La Fontaine.   Open! ye gates of heaven!
And ye good angels, be his convoy thither!
To waft him on melodious waves of air
Beyond our sight.

> [*Angelic strains are heard dying away in the distance.*

   Farel.   So dies he as he lived,
Victorious in faith.

END OF THE DRAMA.

Pp. 93 and 94 of this copy have been revised and amended by the Author.

NOTES

TO

THE REFORMER OF GENEVA.

NOTES.

THE story of the Reformation in Geneva abounds in dramatic materials. The author became impressed by them while engaged in a purely historical investigation, and has simply recast the results of his studies in the literary form here presented. He is not aware that any similiar attempt has been made. A tragical episode has been detached and travestied in German, French, and Spanish ; but no dramatic rendering of the whole story, with due regard to the chief actor, has appeared in any language. It is possible that a more historical treatment would secure artistic completeness as well as moral instructiveness. As a mere dramatic figure Calvin is as impressive as Becket or Richelieu, and the current estimate of Servetus, as well as of Calvin, may be favorably modified by restoring them both to their original environment with an idealization based upon fact and probability. These notes, therefore, are appended in order to verify the strictly historical portions of the drama.

In distinction from the great mass of controversial histories, two works may be selected as the most accessible, as well as authoritative and free from prejudice. One was a memoir contributed to the Historical Society of Geneva by Rilliet de Candolle, professor in the University, who had access to public archives recently discovered, and narrated the trial of Servetus, not only with judicial fairness but with seeming disregard of theological considerations. The other was written by the philosophical historian Guizot, a discriminating critic, who in his sketch of " St. Louis and Calvin," endeavored to harmonize all that is best in Catholicism and Protestantism. These two writers agree substantially in regard to any controverted incidents that appear in the plot. At the same time, by dramatic license, the opinions of enemies as well as friends of the Reformer are fully expressed in the dialogue, often in their own language ; and some expressions, which may have been falsely attributed to both parties, are not withheld, but only discussed in these notes. It need scarcely be added that events are sometimes grouped or blended in accordance with the limitations of dramatic composition ; but their essential significance is not changed.

The original documents, upon which the work of Rilliet is based, are included in the *Corpus Reformatorum*, Calvini Opera, Brunswick ed., vol. viii. They have been carefully studied in reference to every fact, incident, and opinion.

DRAMATIS PERSONÆ.

The chief characters are real with one exception, and may be found more or less clearly delineated by contemporary writers and historians.

AMI PERRIN, military chief of the republic, was the popular leader of the Patriots or native Genevese who resisted the Reformer as a foreigner and innovator. At first, from political motives, in the conflict for independence with the bishop-dukes of Savoy, he espoused the Reformation, and had even advocated the recall of Calvin from banishment ; but when his wife and father-in-law were condemned by the Consistory for serious moral delinquencies his rage became extreme ; and from that day there followed a war of extermination in which Calvin was conqueror only in consequence of the final expulsion of Perrin and his party. Audin, his most favorable critic, describes him as " a man of noble nature, who wore the sword with great grace, dressed in good taste, and conversed with much facility ; but a boaster at table and at the Council, where he deafened everyone with his loquacity, his fits of self-love and his theatrical airs. For the rest, like all men of this stamp, he had an excellent heart, was devoted as a friend, and patriotic to an extreme." In person, he was of swarthy complexion and martial figure.

PHILIBERT BERTHELIER was associated with Perrin, as a chief of the same party, but with somewhat different aims. To him the Reformation was an exotic puritanism. " As a son of one of the martyrs to the political freedom of Geneva," says Rilliet, " his social position and his taste for pleasure gave him the highest rank among the independent and dissipated youth. He was the true *princeps juventutis;* and we find him at the head of all the opposition offered to the austere reforms of Calvin." Gay, astute, cool, and impudent, he was at this time smarting under a sentence of excommunication for his alleged immoralities.

of Geneva.

PIERRE VANDEL, of the same party, was a handsome, brilliant, and frivolous cavalier, who loved to exhibit himself with a retinue of valets and courtesans, with rings on his fingers and golden chains on his breast. He had been imprisoned for his debaucheries and insolent conduct before the Consistory.

CLAUDE DE GENÈVE, the jailer, was an instrument of Perrin; and WILLIAM GUEROULT, an outlawed libertine of the worst class, who had been the printer and proof corrector of the *Christianismi Restitutio*, the heretical book of Servetus.

MICHAEL SERVETUS, a Spaniard of Arragon, physician, geographer, astrologer, litterateur, philosopher, had become known as a fugitive heretic in Germany, Italy, and France. Historians dwell upon his versatile genius and moral inconsistency, as relieved by the sincerity of an enthusiast or the insanity of a fanatic, as well as by pity for his tragical fate and indignation at the reigning intolerance to which he fell a victim. "Many persons," says D'Aubigné, "thought that his subtle understanding, his brilliant genius, his profound knowledge of natural science, would make him one of the most surprising and influential leaders of the epoch." He cannot be reproached with any vices, and though he formed no school, he still has generous defenders. He is described as sensitive, imaginative, acute, of fiery and and fitful temper, often incoherent, and at times with tongue and pen uncontrolled. His frame was slender and delicate, his complexion pale, and his eyes beaming with an expression of melancholy and fanaticism.

JOHN CALVIN, of Noyon in Picardy, humanist, writer, scholar, lawyer, divine, churchman, statesman, was establishing the Reformed faith and discipline in Geneva at a time when it was noted for its unrestrained licentiousness and a turbulence verging upon anarchy. Of commanding intellect and exalted purity, severely just, inflexible, and fearless, he inspired awe rather than popular enthusiasm. His opponents declared that wealth and pleasure had no charms for him. Those who feared him most could easily have destroyed him. Several times he exposed himself to their swords. The city once banished him, but afterwards recalled him in triumph. The public Registers speak of "the majesty of his character." A patrician by education and taste, he was grave and courtly in manner, and though a keen polemic and sometimes truculent after the fashion of that age, yet he was affable among his disciples and friends and at fitting times kindly and tender.

> "Lofty and sour to them that lov'd him not,
> But to those men that sought him, sweet as summer."

In appearance he was of medium size, attenuated in frame, with dark complexion, pointed black beard, chiselled features, large forehead, and piercing eyes that never lost their lustre. His characteristic dress was a broadcloth robe trimmed with fur and a velvet cap of the period.

NICOLAS DE LA FONTAINE, his secretary, was also a Frenchman, who is variously termed his connection, his intimate friend, his disciple, and once his servitor, but in no menial sense, as he is styled by Calvin himself in legal documents "the honorable Nicolas de la Fontaine." In historical paintings he appears with a young, handsome face and intellectual expression.

GERMAIN COLLADON, a French *emigré* of distinguished family and an able jurisconsult, represented the Calvinistic exiles in their conflict with the Libertines and Patriots. Bred to the law, he aided the Reformer in framing the theocratic edicts, becoming a legislator of the puritanical type, with ideas derived from the Mosaic code. He is depicted with a stout figure, massive head and features, and grave magisterial aspect.

WILLIAM FAREL, of noble origin in Dauphiny, was pastor of Neufchâtel, and a devoted friend of the Reformer, whom he had urged to undertake the Reformation of Geneva. He was a popular leader, eloquent, passionate, impetuous, of indomitable courage, whether he harangued evil-doers from the pulpit or faced an angry mob in the streets. Though uncouth in appearance, he had a sonorous voice with the stentorian tones of the orator. POUPIN and BERNARD were Genevan pastors and colleagues of CALVIN, who were of inferior ability.

DU PAN led the Calvinists in the Senate, as VANDEL led the Perrinists, while the Syndic, D'ARLOD, presiding in the absence of the chief Syndic, led the majority as actuated by political rather than religious motives.

FRANCESCA, the daughter of François Favre and wife of the Captain-General Perrin, belonged to one of the old families of Geneva,

of Geneva.

whose gay and dissolute manners were in conflict with the ascetic discipline of the Reformation. The Roman Catholic historian, Audin, characterizes her "as one of those women whom our own Corneille would have taken for heroines; excitable, choleric, fond of pleasure, enamored of dancing, and hating Calvin as Luther hated a monk."

IDELETTE is an ideal personification of the spirit of reformed Geneva, not improbable in the circumstances. As the daughter of Francesca, affianced to La Fontaine, she may represent the blending of the old and new *régime*. The same name was borne by Calvin's wife, Idelette de Bure, who had died several years before the time of the action.

The minor personages and accessory characters are such as appear in the histories of the period. Legal usages and incidents are based upon the contemporary treatise of Bonnivard (*De l'ancienne et nouvelle Police de Genève*) as explained by Rilliet.

ACT I.

NOTE 1—Page 6.

The Consistory was an ecclesiastical court, composed of the five city pastors and twelve laymen, with a Syndic presiding. It had cognizance only of moral and religious offences, but under the Church-State system referred them in some cases to the civic court or Senate for punishment by fine, imprisonment, banishment, or death, according to the degree of the offence.

NOTE 2—Page 6.

The costume of the Genevese at this time had become excessively gay and grotesque, and the sumptuary laws passed at the instigation of the Consistory were trivial and irritating, prescribing in detail the dress of men and women. For example, it was enacted "That no man, in what state, qualitie or condition soever he might be, dareth be so hardie as to make, or cause to be made, or to wear hosen or doublettes cut, jagged, embroydered, or lined with silk, upon payne to forfeyte sixty sous." Calvin refers to the "slashed breeches as a mere piece of foppery not worth speaking about, had it not been a pretext for the most serious disorders."

The entire dialogue between Francesca, Perrin, and Berthelier is founded upon actual incidents as exaggerated by the opponents and critics of the Reformer. "I do not condemn amusements as such," said he; "dances and cards are not in themselves evil, but how easily these pleasures succeed in making slaves of those who are addicted to them! Wherever wrong-doing has become an old-established custom we must avoid every risk of falling back into it." In like manner he opposed the licentious stage of the time, though favoring academic and moral drama under a censorship, and in one instance even postponing his sermon, that the people might attend the theatricals. Yielding at length to the stricter views of his colleagues the magistrates refused to sanction any further representations "until the time was more favorable for them." So far from discountenancing all games he did not scruple himself to play the *Keys* with the Seigneurs of Geneva, a game somewhat like billiards, which consisted in pushing the keys as near as possible to the edge of the table.

NOTE 3—Page 7.

In his conversation and correspondence Calvin veiled his allusions to Madame Perrin under fictitious names characteristic of her improprieties, such as *Penthesilea*, the queen of the Amazons, who led the Trojans in battle against the Greeks; *prodigiosa furia*, a prodigious fury, and *Bacchante* or *Venus dansante*. In like manner he called the Captain-General *Cæsar comicus* or *Cæsar tragicus*, in reference to his love of authority and theatrical effect, as he posed in a sportive or serious humor before the public.

NOTE 4—Page 8.

"In consequence of bacchanalian conduct, Madame Perrin was imprisoned for several days, and from that time the cordial friendship which had united her husband to the Reformer was replaced by implacable hatred."—*Guizot.*

NOTE 5—Page 8.

The power of the Keys, or ecclesiastical right of excommunication, which had been exercised by the ducal bishop, was now claimed by his successor, the civic magistrate, and became the crucial point upon which the whole Reformation turned in Geneva.

of Geneva.

Note 6—Page 9.

"Ami Perrin proposed to take all arms from the French refugees, except their swords, which they were no longer to be allowed to wear in public. Some days later he went a step further, and demanded that the refugees should also be deprived of their swords."—*Guizot*.

Note 7—Page 9.

"It is necessary to describe the position which Perrin and his adherents mentioned under the name of Libertines, held in Geneva, because their hostility to the Reformer, enabling Servetus to meet such powerful allies at the side of his redoubtable opponent, probably drew him to Geneva, and turned his trial into an episode in the struggle which distracted the republican city."—*Rilliet*.

"When Servetus entered Geneva, the Libertines had some reason to expect that they might triumph; one of their leaders, Ami Perrin, was first Syndic:—a man of their party, Gueroult, who had been banished from Geneva, had been corrector of the press at the time when the *Restoration of Christianity* was published, and thanks to the influence of his patrons the Libertines, he had returned to Geneva, and would naturally be the medium between them and Servetus. Taking a comprehensive view of the whole case and the antecedents of all those concerned in it, I am convinced that Servetus, defeated at Vienne, went to Geneva, relying on the support of the Libertines, whilst they on their side expected to obtain efficacious help from him against Calvin."—*Guizot*. See also *Plainte contre Servet* and the evidence at the trial.

Michelet, describing himself as a partisan of Servetus, declares: "Servetus counted on the victory of the Libertines, and it was for this that he prolonged in Geneva the sojourn which caused his destruction."

Note 8—Page 10.

There were several types or degrees of Libertinism in the city. The political Libertines (*enfans de Genève*) were advocates of civil freedom, who had formerly espoused the Reformation, but now resisted it as a foreign intrusion because it sought to abolish the claim of the Senate to the right of absolution, and thus interfered with that impunity in vice which many hoped to secure. The intellectual Libertines (*hérétiques*) might be claimed as advocates of free thought, had they not themselves maintained the right of the State to persecute, and only denied it when they became its victims by their own seditious actions. The spiritual Libertines (*spirituels*) would now be classed as advocates of free love, who under pretense of spiritual affinities and with a blasphemous abuse of Scripture language practiced an adulterous commerce of the sexes. "Their tenets" says Guizot, "were soon made known at Geneva, where they obtained prompt recognition from the local and practical Libertines." These last, the practical Libertines, were the worst class, who had turned the freedom of the Reformation into licentiousness, even choosing a *regina meretricium* and parading the streets with midnight masquerades, indecent songs, and bacchanalian orgies. The different forms of Libertinism shaded into one another, and all its factions at length conspired with Servetus against Calvin.

NOTE 9—Page 11.

The Corinthian portico which now forms the front of the ancient Gothic edifice of St. Peter was not erected until the eighteenth century, more than a hundred years after the Reformation, when the influence of Calvin had waned before that of Rousseau and Voltaire.

NOTE 10—Page 11.

A simile often used by Servetus in his controversial letters and writings.

NOTE 11—Page 12.

"According to his own declaration Servetus kept himself carefully concealed, that he might not be recognized, waiting an opportunity to procure a boat to Zurich and thence to reach the Kingdom of Naples. But notwithstanding this assertion, it is probable that in the inn where he preserved his incognito, he was not without some communication with his allies in the city. If we may believe a contemporary narrative, he had taken a fancy to be present at a sermon preached in one of the churches, and it was there he was discovered."—*Rilliet*.

NOTE 12—Page 15.

"He said he wanted a boat across the lake, so that he might go on to Zurich. He did not cross the lake, but stayed for twenty-seven days at Geneva, greatly exciting the curiosity of his host, who asked him one day if he was married. 'No,' said he, 'there are plenty of women in the world without marrying.'"—*Guizot*.

of Geneva.

NOTE 13—Page 15.

Among the manuscripts of the Reformer in the Library of Geneva is a folio entitled: *Letters par Divers Rois, Princes, Seigneurs, et Dames pour le Consulter sur les cas de Conscience Epineaux, ou pour le Remercier de ses Ouvrages.*

The examples here taken from his correspondence bear upon the time and issue of the action.

NOTE 14—Page 15.

"I do not hesitate to affirm, that the great Catholic bishops who in the seventeenth century directed the conscience of the mightiest men in France did not fulfil this difficult task with more Christian firmness, intelligent justice, fine knowledge of the world, than Calvin displayed in his intercourse with the Duchess of Ferrara."—*Guizot.*

"How was it," asks Renan, "that one of the most distinguished women of her time, René of France, in her court at Ferrara, surrounded by the flower of European wits, was captivated by that stern master, and by him drawn into a course that must have been so thickly strewn with thorns. This kind of austere seduction is exercised by those only who work with real conviction."

NOTE 15—Page 16.

The sect of Libertines prevailed not only in Geneva, but among the higher classes of France and even at the court of Queen Marguerite of Navarre, who countenanced them without adopting their practices.

NOTE 16—Page 17.

"O Philip Melancthon! .... A hundred times, when worn out with labors and oppressed with so many troubles, didst thou repose thy head familiarly on my breast and say, 'Would that I could die on this bosom.'"—*Calvin in An Apostrophe to Melancthon.*

"I give thanks to the Son of God, who was the $B\rho\alpha\beta\epsilon\upsilon\tau\eta s$ [the awarder of your crown of victory] in this your combat."—*Melancthon in a Letter to Calvin.*

NOTE 17—Page 18.

"He offers to come hither, if it be agreeable to me. But I am unwilling to pledge my word for his safety; for if he does come and my authority be of any avail, I shall never suffer him to depart alive."

This sentiment occurs in a private letter to Farel or Viret, which was attributed to the Reformer long after his death. If genuine, it was a well-meant, salutary threat which for seven years had prevented the tragedy at length precipitated by the victim himself.

On the same day, when this alleged letter was written, he wrote to the publisher, Frellen, their common friend, that he despaired of doing Servetus any good by discussion, unless God should change his heart. "But," he adds, "we too ought to lend a helping hand. If God give such grace to him and to us that the present answer will turn to his profit, I shall have cause to rejoice."

Note 18—Page 19.

"In a case demanding corporal punishment, if a party pursue, the said party pursuing must become a prisoner himself and subject himself *ad pœnam talionis*, etc., according to the text of our franchises."—Ordonnances of 1529.

The *Lex Talionis* was based upon the Mosaic code in Exodus xxi., 24, as well as in Leviticus xxiv., 20, and also in the civil codes of Southern Europe.

"It was necessary that there should be a formal accusation and prosecutor who consented to submit to imprisonment and to hold himself criminally responsible for the truth of the charge. Nicolas de la Fontaine, a French refugee, his secretary and intimate friend, consented to take the painful office."—*Guizot*.

Note 19—Page 20.

The seal of the Reformer bore this emblem, with the motto "Cor meum Domino in sacrificium offero." In several emergencies he alludes to its significance.—*See pp.* 20, 35, 87, 89.

When reproached with childlessness by the calumniator Baldwin, the Reformer replied: "God gave me a little son (filiolum), and took him away; but I have myriads of spiritual children in the whole Christian world."

Note 20—Page 21.

"Good God! to what tragedies will not these questions give occasion in times to come."—A sentiment of Melancthon, writing in reference to Servetus.

of Geneva.

ACT II.

Note 1—Page 25.

"In spite of the ecclesiastical ordinances a grand ball had been given, accompanied by excesses in which several of the most important families in the city took part; among others that of the Syndic Ami Perrin, who had at one time been one of Calvin's adherents. A memoir still exists which gives a detailed account of these extraordinary amusements, and from this terrible record it appeared that the dances then performed in private houses would not be tolerated at the present day in the height of the most disorderly carnival."—*Guizot.*

Note 2—Page 25.

"It was his delight to imitate the Reformer, elongating his visage, winking his eyes, and assuming the air of an anchorite of the Thebaid."—*Audin.*

Note 3—Page 27.

All these incidents are historical, and at the time were more serious than amusing. Jacques Gruet, the author of the placard, was beheaded for the worst crimes, as well as for blasphemy.

Note 4—Page 31.

Perrin, his wife, and her father had incurred the censure of the Consistory and been imprisoned for a few days in April, 1546, in consequence of a disgraceful scene of debauchery in which they participated. Favre refused to make any confession, and went to prison, shouting, "Liberty! Liberty!" Perrin made an humble apology to the Consistory.

The victim of the *amende honorable* was obliged to parade through the streets in his shirt, bare-headed, with a lighted torch in his hand, and to ask pardon of the Senate on bended knees.

Note 5—Page 34.

"The Prisoner of Chillon," celebrated in verse by Byron without full knowledge of his character, was François Bonnivard, Prior of St. Victor, the heroic defender of Geneva against the Duke of Savoy. After remaining six years in the dungeon of the Castle of Chillon, an island fortress at the eastern end of the lake, he was restored to liberty by the confederate Bernese forces and became the idol and benefactor of the city. He was a friend of Calvin and favorable to the Reformation, although in one instance he fell under censure of the Consistory because he had played at dice for a quart of beer with Clément Marot, the Huguenot poet.

The Reformer mentions in one of his letters the merriment occasioned by the fourth marriage of Bonnivard. But he was much chagrined when Farel married a young girl after having lived as a bachelor until he was more than seventy years old.

NOTE 6—Page 34.

"Spero capitale saltem fore judicium; pœnæ vero atrocitatem remitti cupio."—*Letter of Calvin, August 20, 1553.*

All the incidents and many expressions in this dialogue are taken from the Reformer's correspondence, and may be found in the biographies of Beza, Henry, D'Aubigné, Guizot, and the Brunswick edition of his Opera.

"Shall I go to Geneva in order to be better off? Shall I not rather go to the cross? To die at once is better than again in that place of torture to suffer a living death."—*Letter to Viret.*

"But since it is not I that decide this case, I offer my bleeding heart a sacrifice to God."—*Letter to Farel.*

"I would rather die than allow myself to be nailed again to that cross, where my blood would flow daily from a thousand wounds."—*Letter to Frellen.*

"I protest that I so much desire the welfare of the Genevan Church, I am ready to suffer a hundred deaths rather than by abandoning betray them."—*Letter to Farel.*

"You see that insolent heretic, Jerome Bolsec, who, though often convicted, has never yet returned to reason; the clemency of the judges, rather than equity, diverting them from their duty, has not merely injured him, but very many more."—*Reply of Farel.*

The letter of Farel makes it clear that he preferred the death penalty for Servetus, and was dissuading Calvin from banishment as mistaken leniency in the case of Bolsec. Farel afterwards, before the execution, pleaded for a milder form of the death penalty, and could scarcely have here advocated the atrocity of burning, if that be at any time conceivable as his meaning.—*See Calvini Opera,* viii., 254.

of Geneva.

Note 7—Page 36.

The Reformer concluded his correspondence with Servetus in these words: "Neither now, nor at any future time, will I mix myself in any way with your wild dreams. Forgive me for speaking thus, but truth compels me to do so. I neither hate you, nor despise you; I do not wish to treat you harshly; but I must be made of iron if I could hear you rail against the doctrine of salvation and not be moved by it."—*Guizot.*

"Why is so implacable a severity exacted but that we may know that God is defrauded of his Honor, unless the piety that is due to Him be preferred to all human duties, and that when His glory is to be asserted, humanity must be almost obliterated from our memories."—*From the Treatise on the Right to Repress Heresy with the Sword. See also Letter to Zurkinda, State Secretary of Berne.*

There can be no doubt that the Reformer, in the spirit of that age, was actuated by high religious motives, which were in conflict with his humane impulses. It was only after his enemies were hypocritically making a saintly martyr of the unfortunate victim, that he was provoked into some ungenerous expressions which have injured his fame more than anything he actually did or said during the trial.

Note 8—Page 37.

In his letter to Cardinal Sadolet, when banished to Strasburg, he avowed that he could never cease to love as his own soul that Geneva which God had entrusted to him.

ACT III.

Note 1—Page 41.

"Servet en prison avait six anneaux d'or; une grande turquoise, un saphir, une table de diamants, rubis, émeraude, anneau de coralline à cacheter, une chaine d'or de seize pouces, deux obligations à 97 ecus, qui représentaient aujourd 'hui 30,000 francs de notre monnaie."—*Audin.*

Note 2—Page 42.

This malediction occurs at the close of his first treatise: "Perdat Dominus omnes ecclesiae tyrannos."

NOTE 3—Page 43.

"Perrin being restored, the malignity of the wicked rose to such a height that some of them openly used collars cut into the form of a cross for the purpose of mutual recognition."—*Beza.*

NOTE 4—Page 43.

"Perrin and his friends, Peter Vandel and Berthelier, determined on rule or ruin, concocted a desperate and execrable conspiracy which at length proved their ruin. They proposed to kill all foreigners who had fled to Geneva for the sake of religion, together with their Genevese sympathizers, on a Sunday while people were at church."—*Schaff.*

NOTE 5—Page 45.

"He must have been informed of events transpiring outside of his prison by some powerful friends. The jailer, named Claude de Genève, a member of the Libertine party and devoted to its leaders, was probably the medium by which Perrin and Berthelier availed themselves (if they were not so employed in person) to convey to Servetus, whether for his sake or their own, directions which tended more and more to embarrass their common enemy."—*Rilliet.*

NOTE 6—Page 45.

It was one of his fancies, amounting at times to a delusion, that he was a warrior of St. Michael, if not St. Michael himself, in the battle with Antichrist, which was represented to him by the Reformers as well as Catholics.

NOTE 7—Page 47.

"The year 1553, and on Monday, the 14th day of August, pursuant to the criminal action raised at the instance of the honorable Nicolas de la Fontaine, of St. Gervais au Vixen, a Frenchman, an inhabitant of this city, against M. Servetus of Villeneuve, in the kingdom of Arragon, in Spain," etc.—*Requête de N. de la Fontaine.*

In this Act the evidence and the argument in the trial are produced substantially in the order of events, together with the reported sayings of the various actors, who figured in the proceedings. Some portions of the text, though historically essential to a full record, may not be found dramatically important in any recitation or representation.

of Geneva.

Note 8—Page 47.

'The public indignation was great, especially in Lyons and Geneva, the former the centre of Catholicism, and the latter of Protestantism."—*Guizot.*

Note 9—Page 49.

This charge is still repeated by some modern critics. Calvin himself denied it most emphatically. It is explained and refuted by Guizot.

Note 10—Page 49.

Heresy was supposed to involve immorality and vice. Servetus had exposed himself to such charges; but declared that he suffered from a hernia, which made him incompetent for libertinage.

Note 11—Page 49.

"It was manifest from the explanations by the publisher [Arnoulet], and the part acted by Gueroult in the printing-house, that the latter must have been in habitual connection with the author."

"The perseverance of Servetus in denying that fact is a distinct proof of its reality; and his conduct cannot be explained, except by the fear which he felt lest they should establish between his connection with the Genevese corrector and his own subsequent visit to Geneva an agreement which might disclose the motive of his coming."—*Rilliet.*

"He was sincere enough in his adhesion to his own views, but on other points they found him frivolous, vain, arrogant, irresolute and untruthful. He denied any connection, even the most indirect, not only with the Libertines of Geneva, but with their agent, Gueroult, at Geneva, who had corrected the proofs of his book."—*Guizot.*

Note 12—Page 50.

"The interposition of Berthelier in favor of Servetus is established by the registers of the Council. Besides, the protection held out by Berthelier to Servetus is notorious—two contemporaries, Roset and Beza, expressly declared it. It was the natural result of their common hostility to the Reformer, and we have here the first indication of the support given to the prisoner by the Libertine party."—*Rilliet.*

The Reformer

Note 13—Page 50.

Ceasing to conceal himself behind La Fontaine and Colladon, Calvin became for the first time openly the accuser of the prisoner; and added that he learned by the process that Berthelier had interfered to plead in excuse and defence of those things which the said Servetus had consented to name as established by his book."—*Rilliet.*

Note 14—Page 51.

"Upon the request of Colladon, the Court finding by the proof and facts, produced on the part of the pursuer, that Servetus clearly appeared to be guilty, resolved immediately to liberate De la Fontaine."—*Rilliet.*

The charges upon which Servetus was actually tried and at length condemned were not drawn up by the Reformer, nor by Colladon, but by the public prosecutor, Rigot, on behalf of the city, and referred less to the moral offences of heresy and blasphemy than to the strictly political crimes of sedition and conspiracy, evidence of which accumulated during the trial, as the plot of the Libertines was brought to light. See Articles du Procureur-général. Requisitoire du Procureur-général.

Note 15—Page 51.

Calvin and his colleagues were now retained as experts rather than as parties in the case, dogmatic questions being naturally beyond the competence of the civic court: "Ces matières n' étant naturellement pas de la compétence des members ordinaires du tribunal."

Note 16—Page 52.

Two points were very well taken and defended by Servetus. He prayed first that he might be freed from a criminal charge; and second, that if not thus liberated, being a foreigner, he might have the aid of an advocate who knew the laws and procedure of the country. In support of the former request he urged that the primitive Church did not treat heresy as a criminal offence before a civil tribunal, nor impose any worse penalty than banishment upon a heretic who would not repent. The whole petition, in the light of our times, seems moderate and reasonable, and exceedingly well put against a charge of heresy as distinguished from one of mere sedition.

Note 17—Page 52.

Servetus attacked Calvin still more keenly as instigator of the prosecution at Vienne, emboldened by the presence of Berthelier and Vandel who shared the same hostile feeling. He also offered to show in a public discussion with Calvin, by proofs from reason and Holy Scripture, that his opinions were not injurious to the Church of Geneva, nor contrary to sound doctrine. By this bold manœuvre he might have gained a popular following and turned some of the factions against his adversary. Calvin promptly accepted the challenge, declaring that there was "nothing he more desired than to plead such a cause in the temple before all the people." But the Syndics would not permit the debate, some being jealous of their judicial prerogative, and others fearing that their *protégé* might be worsted in such an encounter.

Note 18—Page 53.

Rilliet tells us that the Attorney-General had become convinced that the prisoner was already self-condemned, and indignantly denied his request for an advocate as inept and impertinent; because he knew so well how to lie that no procurator could help him in his falsehoods; because there was not a jot of innocence in the case to require an attorney, and because the statutes would not allow such seducers to speak by counsel.

Note 19—Page 54.

The language of Bullinger, one of the most temperate of the Reformers.

Note 20—Page 54.

A sentiment of Bucer, said to have been uttered from the pulpit.

Note 21—Page 54.

While the trial was passing in the Bishop's palace the greatest excitement prevailed in the city. The proceedings were watched with keen interest. The factions were taking sides for and against the prisoner. In the Great Council of Two Hundred, a popular assembly then largely hostile to Calvin, the theatrical Perrin and the fascinating Berthelier were mustering their followers, not so much in sympathy with Servetus and his opinions as with the design of using him as a tool in crushing the Reformer and his hated discipline. On the other hand, Calvin and the pastors were rallying their people in defence of sound doctrine and pure discipline, and thundering from the pulpit against the horrible impieties of the heretic Spaniard as well as his seditious connections with the Libertine party. The whole city was in a ferment and on the verge of a revolution. At length the conflict found expression in the Council itself. Such scenes of disorder were not unusual at this time even in the Senate Chamber.

NOTE 22—Page 55.

"Méchant homme, vous voulez boire le sang de notre famille, mais vous sortirez de Genève avant nous."

NOTE 23—Page 55.

These epithets are but a selection from others preserved in the archives of the trial, such as *nebulo, Simon Magus, impostor, sychophanta, perfidus, impudens, ridiculus mus, cacodæmon, homicida.* In his last written argument the word *mentiris* (thou liest) occurs repeatedly as in the ravings of a madman. After the outburst of passion Calvin made no further replies. Guizot tells us that the prisoner disgusted and shocked the judges by his brawling invectives. The charitable judgment now would be that he was more insane than culpable.

NOTE 24—Page 56.

"Calvin answered: If there were as many crowns as there are empty heads in your family, you would not be able to change the current of ecclesiastical discipline. Your efforts to shake off the yoke of the Gospel will be in vain."—*Guizot.*

NOTE 25—Page 57.

"It is our duty to fight so much the more valiantly when we are under the eye of the Great Judge of combats, who dwelleth in the highest heavens. What! that holy and glorious band of angels, who promise us their favor, will they leave us without strength to drag our limbs to the grave? Still more the Church of God, which is in this world, and which we know strives with us by prayer and is encouraged by our example,—shall its voice and its sympathy have no weight with us? Let this then be my theatre; with the approbation which it accords me I shall be more than satisfied, though all the world should tear me in the face."—*Letter to the Queen of Navarre.*

NOTE 26—Page 57.

"As to the right to inflict punishment for the errors of religious opinion, and to chastise impiety, that was never a question in the mind of the magistrate. In condemning Servetus and his doctrines, the Senate did not think that it was doing aught more strange than in declaring Berthelier capable of receiving the Communion."—*Rilliet*.

Note 27—Page 58.

The arms of Geneva then displayed the imperial eagle impaled with the keys, representing the combined powers of the State and the Church.

Note 28—Page 59.

" The opposition of the Council in favor of Berthelier," says Rilliet, " had turned the head of Servetus." Borne aloft amid the general excitement, he mistook his chance prominence for a personal following in the city as well as in the Council. His tone became defiant and aggressive. No longer the meek, plausible suppliant that he was a month ago, he heaped upon Calvin, as upon a fallen foe, epithets more virulent than any he had ever before devised, and eagerly joined against him in the appeal to the Bernese government. Indeed, backed as he supposed by the whole Libertine faction, he even dreamed of supplanting the Reformer in Geneva; denounced him as an impostor who ought to be hunted from the city, and invoking that civil arm which he had before deprecated, he appeared before the Council as the accuser of his accuser; demanded that Calvin be put on trial as a prisoner with him, " until the cause be decided for his death or mine," by the law of retaliation; and concluded his petition with a formal list of " articles on which M. Servetus wishes J. Calvin to be interrogated." Nor was the poor deluded man altogether astray in some of his conjectures. It is quite certain that had the Council in its present temper, as led by the chief Syndic, proceeded to a decision, Servetus would have been released and Calvin might have suffered death or exile in his place. This result was yet to be prevented by the very stratagem which had been devised to produce it. For the present, however, the parties have come to a pause, and must await the decision of the tribunal to which they have appealed.

Note 29—Page 60.

" Even the Senate had arrived at that pitch of rage and madness that were we to declare it is day at high noon they would immediately begin to doubt it."—*Calvin to Bullinger*.

The Reformer

Note 30—Page 60.

On the 21st of August, the Senate passed the following order: " Inasmuch as the case of the heresy of M. Servetus vitally affects the welfare of Christendom, it is resolved to proceed with his trial; and also to write to Vienne to know why he was in prison, and how he escaped; and after that, when all is ascertained, to write to the magistrates of Berne, of Basel, of Zurich, of Schaffhausen and of other churches of the Swiss, to acquaint them with the whole."

"Ceasing to be a local trial, the cause of Servetus was about to become the affair of the Swiss Reformation."—*Rilliet.*

ACT IV.

Note 1—Page 64.

The great bell in the lofty tower of St. Peter, a gift of Bishop De Lornay, was called "Clémence" after Clement VII., the antipope, and on great occasions sent its deep tones far and wide over the city and the neighboring valleys.

" A music-master who was paid by the State, gave three lessons a week to several choirs of children. When they had learned the psalm thoroughly, they sang it during the service."—*Guizot.*

The Psalms, as translated by Clément Marot and edited by Calvin and Beza, became the favorite songs of the Huguenots throughout France, even at the court of Margaret of Navarre. The historian, Douen, claims that the Reformer, by thus popularizing sacred music, became one of the fathers of the opera or lyric drama.

Note 2—Page 68.

The state of parties had somewhat changed during the past month. There was a reaction in public feeling. The prisoner had never had any enthusiastic support. The two partisan senators had no further use for him and he had lost the sympathy of the judges by his fits of rage and insolence. He continued to petition them from his prison for more humane treatment, which was granted him, but without further discussion. He must have felt the doom which was impending, and when at last the State Messenger returned with the adverse decision, the illusion which for a time had brightened his prison was gone. Weakened in body and broken in spirit, he sought refuge, says Rilliet, in the first asylum opened to the undeceived, namely, in despair, striking his breast, like one demented, and with loud groans that resounded through the prison exclaiming in Spanish, "Mercy!" "Mercy!" By degrees he recovered his composure, but had lost his passion and his pride.

NOTE 3—Page 69.

Servetus, among his medical researches, conjectured, if he did not discover, the circulation of the blood, which nearly a hundred years afterwards was verified and completed by Harvey, who probably had no knowledge of the speculations of the Spanish physician.

NOTE 4—Page 69.

"He was left under the custody of Jehanton Gerod, the sheriff, and Peter Costel, of the Council of Sixty; probably to prevent the attempts which the jailer, Claude de Genève, who, we have said, was in the confidence of Perrin, and an enemy of the Calvinists, might have planned in his favor."—*Rilliet.*

NOTE 5—Page 69.

After the sentence was found to be imminent and the judges inexorable, the only hope of saving Servetus was by inducing him to recant. The execution still hung upon that condition, and it was the prevailing theory of such punishments that a true believer would renounce his errors while under discipline. In the hope of such a result, by the desire of Calvin, Farel visited the prison early the next morning. But the prisoner was more argumentative than penitent. He insisted upon having Scriptural proof of the eternal Sonship of Christ, whom he still acknowledged in some sense as his Saviour. The passages cited did not convince him, or shake his constancy. Farel persuaded him to request an interview with Calvin, and the latter came, attended by the Syndics Corné and Bonna, as witnesses to the recantation which they hoped to secure. Sixteen years ago, when he first met Servetus at Paris, he had endeavored, at the risk of his own life, as he said, "to cure him of his madness, and bring him to such sentiments that all pious men might take him affectionately by the hand."

NOTE 6—Page 71.

For a description of this whole scene see Rilliet and Guizot. It has been well said that the last hours of Servetus were the best of his life. Sobered in view of eternity, he lost his pride, conceit, and passion, and the latent good in him gained control. Though not a saint or martyr, in the usual sense of the terms, his acts and words became Christian. " The dignity of the philosopher," says Guizot, "triumphed over the weakness of the man, and Servetus died heroically and calmly at that stake, the very thought of which had at first filled him with terror."

NOTE 7—Page 73.

This incident is fully described by Beza, Rilliet, and Guizot. Schaff characterizes it as a "sublime triumph of reason over passion."

NOTE 8—Page 66.

"A heretic," says John Knox, " if he suffers the death pronounced by a lawful magistrate, is not persecuted for his conscience (as in the name of Servetus ye furiously complain), but he suffereth punishment according to God's commandment pronounced in Deuteronomy, the 13th chapter."

The learned jurist, Sir J. D. Michaelis, in his "Commentaries on the Laws of Moses," defended the civil punishment of false teaching and blasphemy, not merely as being sins against God but crimes against the peace of society and the rights of individuals, and only deprecated the capital penalty, on the ground that it might give the offender too much prominence and excite public sympathy for his fate.

NOTE 9—Page 73.

" The factions had ruined themselves by their own hands, a dreadful conspiracy having been very opportunely discovered, through the petulant audacity of certain of the conspirators when in a state of drunkenness."—*Beza.*

NOTE 10—Page 74.

The Senate was not a unit, and for some time wavered, as if reluctant to face the issue. The chief Syndic Perrin, day after day feigned illness and stayed away from court. At length, the prisoner having been duly informed and more strictly guarded, a final sitting was ordered for the 26th of October, in joint session with the Council of Sixty, without whose concurrence they could not legally pass sentence. It was a full meeting, and the debate was high and stormy. The Captain-General, after some last ineffectual efforts to

of Geneva.

acquit the prisoner or transfer his case to the Great Council, left the Senate chamber with his followers, defeated and disgusted.

Note 11—Page 76.

The correspondence with Vienne was based upon the common interest of Catholics and Protestants in a heresy which, it was thought, destroyed the very foundations of Christianity. It was begun on the part of the Senate by sending a messenger of state into Dauphiny with letters to the magnificent and noble lords, the judges of the court of Vienne, requesting a copy of the evidence and information against Servetus, to be used in bringing him to that just punishment from which he had escaped. Nine days afterwards, August 31st, came a reply to the most noble, wise, and illustrious lords, the Syndics and Senate of Geneva, saying that it would be contrary to French law to surrender the papers in a trial against a criminal already sentenced and burned in effigy, and begging that Servetus be returned to them for punishment, and further charges against him be thus avoided. The commandant of the royal palace brought this letter with a copy of the sentence, and a jailer to take the prisoner back with him to Vienne. Servetus was asked if he would return with the jailer or remain in the hands of the Senate. The wretched man could only see the fagots already piled for him in Dauphiny, and falling upon his knees he begged the judges to go on with his trial, promising to submit to their good pleasure. As Genevese law did not allow the extradition of criminals, they ordered a gracious response to be written, that they could not give him up, but would execute full justice upon him ; and the papal officer withdrew, having first obtained a certificate from Servetus that he had escaped from prison through no favor or aid of his keepers. The next day came a letter, written by M. de Maugiron, lieutenant of the King of France, informing the Senate that the goods of the prisoner, amounting to four thousand crowns, had been confiscated, and requesting a statement of his debts and credits. He was protected by his two patrons in refusing such a statement, and the request was politely declined. M. de Maugiron, in closing his letter, complimented the zeal of the Genevese judges, and thanked God that the heretic was now in the hands of those who would not let him again escape punishment. It was thus that Romanist and Protestant authorities became strangely agreed in defence of their common Christianity, as they understood it, and even vied with each

The Reformer

other, according to Killiet, for the dismal privilege of burning Servetus. The records of the first trial of Servetus at Vienne and the subsequent correspondence with the Genevese magistrates are preserved in the archives of the Papal Inquisition at Vienne.

NOTE 12—Page 77.

When the Reformer found that the magistrates were bent upon the extreme penalty, he could only plead for mercy in the execution of the law. With his colleagues he besought them either to change the sentence or effect it in a milder form, perhaps by means of the sword. "We endeavored," he wrote Farel, "to alter the mode of his death, but in vain. Why we did not succeed I defer for narration until I see you." There is no record of that conversation, but it is easy enough to see why they did not succeed. Even if the judges had been disposed to listen to Calvin, they were in no mood for clemency towards the prisoner. He had long since exhausted their patience, not only by his personal traits, but as an irritating source of the public troubles. They could see no extenuation of his guilt; and as he was already under sentence and burned in effigy, they chose to stay within the letter of the statute providing the same penalty which he had a second time defied.

In a subsequent controversy, when accused of cruelty, the Reformer called the two most hostile judges to witness that he had interceded in behalf of Servetus, and had at no time desired his death. —See Opera *ix.*, 315. viii., 463.

NOTE 13—Page 78.

The scene of the sentence is rendered with historical accuracy.

NOTE 14—Page 80.

According to Farel, these were the last words of Servetus, uttered at the stake. They expressed his Christian faith, as distinguished from the theological error for which he had been condemned, which was a denial of the eternal Sonship of Christ.

ACT V.

NOTE 1—Page 83.

The Registers show that a fine of three sous was imposed for non-attendance at sermon, especially on Sunday.

of Geneva.

Note 2—Page 84.

"A peasant was imprisoned because, on hearing an ass bray, he said in jest: ''What a fine psalm he chants!'"

Note 3—Page 84.

"It does not appear that the connection of Servetus with the heads of the opposition had acquired for him any great favor among the masses who were unacquainted with him. The party of the Genevese people who were hostile to Calvin continued unconcerned amid the discussion, which was followed out and concluded in a higher region than theirs. It would have excited their attention had Servetus attracted their sympathies; it met with nothing but indifference, because it was no business of theirs."—*Rilliet.*

Note 4—Page 85.

Berthelier recites the somewhat mythical story of the burning of Servetus as given at the time in an anonymous and hostile tract, *Historia de Morte Serveti.* It is claimed that the green wood and wreath of sulphur were not peculiar to this case, but customary and mercifully designed to hasten death by suffocation.

Note 5—Page 86.

"Shortly after the execution of Servetus, the Libertines raised a demonstration against Farel. Philibert Berthelier and his brother, François Daniel, stirred up the laborers to throw Farel into the Rhone. But his friends formed a guard around him."—*Schaff.*

"A right-hearted young man among the citizens, after warning Perrin to take care that Farel, who was regarded as the common father of the citizens, should suffer no harm, gave information to others who were known to be well affected."—*Beza.*

Guizot tells us that the friends of Calvin vainly tried to keep him away from the scene of tumult. Without their knowledge he went out and walked alone to the Town-Hall, where he was received with outcries and drawn swords.—*See Calvin's "Letter to Viret."*

Note 6—Page 87.

It was a flagrant act of rebellion to seize the Syndic's bâton, which was viewed by the populace as the symbol of civil authority. Perrin vociferated, "The staff is ours! We hold it!"

The Reformer

NOTE 7—Page 88.

All the incidents brought together in this scene actually happened. In describing it the bitterest detractor of the Reformer cannot help paying a tribute to him and to the truth of history.

"Never," says Audin, "had any session been more tumultuous; the parties, weary of speaking, began to appeal to arms. The people heard the appeal. Calvin appears, unattended; he is received with cries of death. He folds his arms and looks the agitators fixedly in the face. Not one of them dares strike him. Then advancing through the midst of the groups, with his breast uncovered: 'If you want blood,' says he, 'there are still a few drops here. Strike, then!' Not an arm is raised. Calvin then slowly ascends the stairway to the Council of the Two Hundred. The hall was on the point of being drenched with blood: swords were flashing. On beholding the Reformer the weapons were lowered, and a few words sufficed to calm the agitation. Calvin, taking the arm of one of the senators, again descends the stairs, and cries out to the people that he wishes to address them. He does speak, and with such energy and feeling that tears flow from their eyes. They embrace each other and the crowd retires in silence. The patriots had lost the day. From that moment it was easy to foretell that victory would remain with the Reformer. The Libertines, who had shown themselves so bold when it was a question of destroying some front of a Catholic edifice, or entering some saint's niche, or throwing down an old wooden cross weakened by age, trembled like women before this man, who, in fact, on this occasion exhibited something of the Homeric heroism."

Guizot, in reference to the same incident, says: "There is sometimes one happy moment in which courage conquers anger. . . . The reaction was as sudden as the explosion. Calvin continued: 'I know that I am the chief cause of your quarrels, and if blood must be shed to appease them, take my life, for I call God to witness that I am come to expose myself to your swords. . . . There is nothing except religion which can make you free and secure your liberty; but in order to obtain this you must be united, and if my presence is an insuperable obstacle to the maintenance of peace, I will, leave the city, and will pray to God that those men who desire to live without Christianity and law may save the republic and maintain its prosperity.'"

of Geneva.

Note 8—Page 89.

Besides his metrical versions of some of the Psalms, Calvin composed at least one hymn, full of devotional fervor and tenderness, "Salutation à Jésus Christ." The verse in the text is founded upon the emblem of his seal, "I offer my heart as a burning sacrifice to God."

Note 9—Page 90.

The sentences of Berthelier and Perrin are recorded in the public Registers. See also *Bayles's* "*Philosophical Dictionary*," article Berthelier.

Note 10—Page 91.

"When a child he was seen joining the religious processions, and carrying a sword with a cross-shaped hilt by way of a crucifix."—*D'Aubigné*.

Contrary to popular impressions, the Reformer with all his moral courage was physically timid and retiring and not without strong affections. After the death of his wife he wrote his most intimate friend, Viret: "You know the tenderness—not to say the weakness—of my heart. I should give way utterly if God had not stretched out His hand to hold me up." The public Registers attest his forgiving disposition as in the cases of Bolsec, Gentilis, and Castello, who only returned his kindness with calumny.

Note 11—Page 93.

Calvin, who shared largely in the humanistic culture of his time, and was a master of pure Latinity, wrote a Latin ode, *Epinicion ad Christum*, or Song of Victory to Christ, celebrating the triumph of the Reformation over its enemies, in classical diction and imagery. It concluded with these lines:

"Magnifico celebrem Christi cantate triumphum
Carmine. *Io Pæan* cætera turba canat."

"Let His head be crowned with the laurel of victory, let Him be seated on a chariot drawn by four coursers abreast, that His glory may shine forth before all. . . . And you, O sacred poets, celebrate in magnificent song the triumph of Christ, and let the multitudes shout *Io Pæan*."

The Reformer of Geneva

NOTE 12—Page 93.

The Reformer several times lamented the "excessive vehemence" which had marked some of his controversies. He alluded to it twice, in his patriarchial dying address to the Syndics and Senators, concluding with these words:

"Finally, I again entreat you to pardon my infirmities, which I acknowledge and confess before God and His angels, and also before you, my much respected Lords."

Having thus spoken, and prayed for the safety of the whole Republic, giving his right hand to each, he left them in sorrow and tears, all feeling as if they were taking a last farewell of their common parent.—*Beza's* "*Life of Calvin.*"

NOTE 13—Page 93.

In accordance with the maxim of his life, "Let my name be unknown or utterly buried—if the truth prevail," he explicitly enjoined that no monument should be put over his grave. To this day the place of his sepulture is not certainly known.

TABLE OF SCENES.

	PAGE
ACT I.—THE PLOT OF THE LIBERTINES	3
Scene I.—The Captain-General's Palace	5
Scene II.—The Doorway of the Cathedral	11
Scene III.—The Same at Curfew	13
Scene IV.—Interior of the Consistory	15
ACT II.—THE COUNTERPLOT OF THE REFORMERS	23
Scene I.—The Garden of the Palace	25
Scene II.—The Same by Moonlight	26
Scene III.—Anteroom in the Palace	30
Scene IV.—Interior of the Consistory	33
ACT III.—THE TRIAL OF SERVETUS	39
Scene I.—A Dungeon in the Old Bishop's Palace	41
Scene II.—A Hall of Justice in the Same	45
ACT IV.—THE JUDGMENT OF CHRISTENDOM	61
Scene I.—A Room in the Captain-General's Palace	63
Scene II.—A Dungeon in the Old Bishop's Palace	68
Scene III.—The Senate Chamber in the Town Hall	72
ACT V.—THE TRIUMPH OF THE REFORMATION	81
Scene I.—The Public Square and Town Hall	83
Scene II.—Before the Cathedral	88
Scene III.—The Interior of the Cathedral	92

www.ingramcontent.com/pod-product-compliance
Lightning Source LLC
Chambersburg PA
CBHW020110170426
43199CB00009B/468